YEONMI PARK
BIOGRAPHY

The Journey Finding Freedom While Time Remains

GW00454865

Lehrae Thomas

"I have lived a life of despair, but I have never given up hope."

Note:

....
....
....
....
....
....
....

TABLE OF CONTENTS

INTRODUCTION
American Bastards

The classroom is run-down and chilly. It smells like the furnace in the corner of the room, where the used wood has broken down into white ash. Black stains cover the wall above the furnace, and the embers crack and burst as the wood falls apart from its own weight. I am virtually indistinguishable from my twenty students since we are all huddled together for warmth on the cold concrete floor, wearing the same worn-out winter outfits. While some of us are famished, others are hungry. A few people battle to stay awake; when they doze off, their heads drop and their eyes roll back.

I believe it is preferable to sleep than to be awake and hungry.

I'm forced to sit with other "struggling" youngsters on the far side of the back row, which is also the one furthest from the furnace. I question why I couldn't do better in school so that I can sit in the front row. I clench my hands and squeeze my eyes shut, hoping it will happen so the teacher will bring me forward and closer to the heat. I find myself still in the back when I open my eyes. Of course, I understand why: I'm a terrible student. I frequently have no idea what my teacher and fellow students are discussing. Math is like learning a foreign language, whereas history is impossible to memorize.

The only way to make up for being a poor student is to exceed the "rabbit pelt quota"—each student is required to deliver five furs per semester, ostensibly for the army's winter uniforms but actually for the school administrators to sell—and to respond to inquiries about our "Socialist Paradise" with an intense, almost hysterical passion. I'm also not very adept at doing these.

I pause, purse my lips, and blink openly. Though the room is now completely dark, I can still smell the burning wood. My pupils and the teacher have left, but I can still hear footsteps shuffling across the concrete floor and whispers. Someone must be present. I turn to the embers in the furnace, which are the only source of light. They appear, vanish, and then come back like flashing lights. In front of the furnace, a person is pacing back and forth.

I hear a loud whistling sound, like artillery. I glance out the window, but all I see is a flare. It illuminates the night sky and floods the classroom with white light. I whirl around to take another look at the furnace.
The man behind two soldiers who are moving toward me with fixed bayonets is hidden. He paces back and forth in front of the furnace while wearing a black suit and tosses a lighted cigar on the ground.
I scream as I awaken.

With my palms flat on the wet sheets and my spine straight as a board, I sit up in bed. I'm in my Morningside Heights, New York City, apartment. Now that I'm secure, I can clearly see that it was all a dream. However, it takes some time for my muscles to unwind and for my body to calm. Nearing 4:00 a.m. Little noise is coming from the street below. Even though my skin is still perspiring, I turn up the heat a little and turn on the lamp.

In 2015, when I immigrated to the United States of America, MY GREATEST dream was fulfilled. I could never have envisioned the conclusion to my North Korean escape in my wildest thoughts. As a part of a volunteer mission program out of Tyler, Texas, which is southeast of Dallas, I had previously visited that location in 2013. Even though I was poor and barely spoke English at the time, I discovered that Americans were very different from what I had been taught as a child and that America was a large and breathtakingly beautiful place.
Even math lessons in North Korean schools typically feature anti-American rhetoric. "Of the five American tanks that were present, the North Korean Army destroyed four. How many remain? Those sorts of things. Furthermore, it would have been perceived as being curiously respectful to simply say "American" without any additional insults. Every time, it was "American bastards," "Yankee devils," or "big-nosed Yankees."

Graphic illustrations were also employed in North Korean classrooms to support the official state narrative about the United

States. Brutal illustrations of blond-haired, green-eyed, and bearded American soldiers killing Korean civilians or being slain by valiant North Korean students brandishing pitchforks and bayonets were plastered all over our textbooks and even some classroom walls. We used to line up in the bitter cold during recess and take turns using sticks that had been whittled into spears to stab dummies of American GIs to keep ourselves sharp for when the enemy would eventually return.

The message was crystal clear: You are all in immediate danger as a result of the genuine and impending threat from America.

I can still vividly recall how terrified I used to be at night that Yankee bastards would bomb and invade Hyesan, kill my parents, and torment Eunmi and I for fun.

Of course, lies about America are just one aspect of the propaganda that is taught in North Korean classrooms. Additionally, we were taught that the Kim dynasty possesses supernatural abilities and that the North Korean people were given their own existence as a gift from Heaven. The founding father of North Korea, Kim Il Sung (1912–1994), was venerated not just as a godlike figure but as a true deity. He was so effective in creating this personality cult that when he passed away from a heart attack, nobody questioned the veracity of his claimed immortality.

Kim Jong Il's (1941–2011) birthday is celebrated as Kwang Myong Song-jol, or "Day of the Shining Star." The night he was born, a dazzling star is said to have arisen in the sky over Paektu Mountain, the highest point in North Korea, and guerilla soldiers are said to have etched signs saying, "Oh! Korea! The Paektu Star Was Born!" onto trees. Additionally, there are "Three Heroes Shining in Korea with the Spirit of Mount Paekdu: Kim Il Sung, Kim Jong-suk [his first wife], and Kwang Myong Song." The "morning star" of Jesus Christ in the Book of Revelation and the "shining star" of Kim Jong Il, the son of North Korea's founding deity, have been compared by numerous observers.

A businessman from Hyesan named Park Jin Sik, My father, dedicated his life to doing anything he could to make things better for his family. He chose to work for himself in the black market after becoming dissatisfied with the meager living he made working at a closed factory. He started by selling cigarettes in the nearby townships and ultimately moved on to smuggling copper and other metals into the adjacent China. Although this type of operation was hazardous, the rewards were worth it. My father was a natural salesman who knew how to get around the law and satisfy his clients. I was seven when we were living a joyful, somewhat prosperous life.

However, when I was nine years old, my father was apprehended by the police and given a hard labor sentence in a camp outside Pyongyang, roughly 550 miles southwest of Hyesan. My mother, Keum Sook Byeon, was regarded as his accomplice and received a prison sentence as well. She endured repeated sexual abuse and interrogations during this time. Because she had moved her home from Hyesan to Kowon without permission, she was ultimately given a lengthy sentence of hard labor. She "disappeared" for up to forty days at a time for nearly two years.

At that time, my thirteen-year-old sister Eunmi and I were left alone in Hyesan and Kowon, the hometown of my mother. It was the most difficult time of my life up to that moment.

After bribing a guard, my mother was eventually allowed to leave jail early. Three years later, in 2006, my father was also allowed to leave the camp after serving three years in a labor camp. Both of them had bribed their respective prison guards in exchange for safe passage to Hyesan and the promise of paying them back when they returned. Finally, we were all back together. However, the joy I had at seeing my father again was soon overshadowed by the knowledge that he had changed. His zest for life had vanished, his mouth lines were trending downward, and his eyes lacked the gleam that had usually lit up his face when he told us tales of his exploits traveling through North Korea on "business," as well as how he'd heard that other nations were "advanceing." (Because I had never seen a map before, I had no idea what this meant.) My father was ill and distraught. In Hyesan, the four of us were back together, but this time we were a different family. We had no longer any chance of ever being whole again.

Although it may be challenging for outsiders to understand, the life of an ex-offender is significantly worse than that of a North Korean "average" person. Like in America or Europe, there are no reintegration programs, case managers, social workers, employment help, or opportunities for reentry. The former inmate from North Korea is a pariah, and his family is responsible by association. They are demoted to the lowest caste and avoided by society. No collective farm, factory, branch of the armed forces, or position in the public service will accept them since their blood is polluted, and the doors to opportunity are shut.

Then Eunmi vanished one night. My parents became worried when she didn't arrive home for several hours and started looking for her all over town. But as the night wore on, it became increasingly clear that Eunmi was no longer in Hyesan; she was no longer merely lost or difficult to find. We eventually discovered a note she had buried under my pillow, stating that she had crossed the Yalu River into China after deciding she couldn't stand our poverty any longer. The note told me to get in touch with a woman who was assisting her outside of town; she would be able to tell me how to get in touch with Eunmi. Her choice produced a lot of resentment and dread in our family because it was incredibly dangerous to both her own life and ours.

To make matters worse, right before Eunmi's escape, I developed severe abdominal discomfort out of the blue and needed to be transported to the hospital. I had surgery with poor anesthetic after receiving a false appendix diagnosis. During the surgery, I woke up and fainted from the pain.

Several days had gone by when I came to the shabby hospital bed. My parents appeared to be on the verge of lunacy, and Eunmi had left.

When I explain that, in some ways, our nightmare just started after we fled North Korea, even the most ardent critics of the Chinese state exhibit shock and horror. My mother and I were sold to different human traffickers in Changbai County, in the southern Chinese province of Jilin, each time for a higher fee. Finally, we were sold as "wives" to rural Chinese men who were unable to obtain a wife from their own country. (The draconian one-child policy of the CCP, enacted in 1980 to control population growth, led to a generation of "missing women" because many Chinese households preferred sons over daughters.) My mother was forty-one years old, and I was thirteen.

Eventually, the man who had me as his mistress made a vow to assist in getting my mother back and even in getting my father to China. He was faithful to his word. I begged for a simple favor like that, but by the time he delivered on his word, I had changed. My perceived remaining sanity and innocence were lost. Eunmi was still nowhere to be found.

My mum and I met again three months later. Three months later, my father finally made it to China, which was bittersweet. The nicest birthday present I could have ever received fell on the same day as my fourteenth birthday, but by that time he was too ill to work. We had no idea what was wrong with him at the time, but we later learned that he had colon cancer, which had gone unrecognized for years while he was incarcerated. After a kind of experimental surgery was performed on him in China, the medical professionals concluded that there was nothing more that could be done because the cancer had spread to most of his body.

My father died at the start of 2008. I was attending to him at the time of his death, holding his lifeless corpse in my arms. I recall that it was 7:30 a.m. and that I had spent the previous evening holding him and trimming his fingernails. Even with my mother seated next to me, I was distraught, indignant, and experienced an unbearable sense of loneliness. Knowing that my father, who had managed to find happiness, excitement, and love despite a life that had been defined by tremendous agony, was no longer experiencing pain was the only thing that could have staved off the utmost darkness. In contrast to the living, he was content.

With the assistance of two goons hired by the man who referred to me as his mistress, my mother and I moved my father's body in the dark. To prevent being caught by Chinese police, it had to be done at night (my "husband" was only permitted to bring in North Korean women, not men). My father was abruptly burnt, so I moved his ashes to the top of a hill overlooking a river in Yangshanzhen to avoid drawing attention. I hastily buried his bones out of concern that if I uttered a prayer word, I would start to cry and the police would hear me, sending me back to North Korea.

The trafficker who had me as his mistress for a year eventually succumbed to a severe gambling addiction. He permitted my mother and I to seek safety elsewhere when he was no longer able to pay for much. A group of Christian missionaries who helped North Korean defectors in China by first converting them and then sending them to South Korea were eventually introduced to us.

The missionaries' route seeking defectors was difficult and entailed nighttime travel over Mongolia's Gobi Desert. A small group of eight people, including a couple with a young child, included my mother and I. We had nothing but the stars and a compass to lead us because we were starving and freezing. We followed the route that our advisors had suggested until we were finally found by a Mongolian border guard. We were moved to a military installation and processed before being dispatched to South Korea.

Since then, I've considered the Gobi Desert to be my personal Red Sea and my means of liberation. On the night we spent traveling through the desert, I can still recall how I felt as I looked up at the sky: incredulous awe, followed by a crushing sense of loneliness and complete insignificance. I remember thinking that when my mother passed away, no one would ever know or care if I passed away that night from frostbite, an illness, or by becoming prey to a wild animal.

To share my tale and the narrative of the 21 million North Koreans still imprisoned in the bleakest place on earth, I had to continue to exist.

We were fortunate to arrive in South Korea unscathed, my mother and I. We were regularly warned by the missionaries who assisted us to be ready in case we were apprehended by Chinese officials and transported back to North Korea. We had only prepared razors and poison as a way of hasty exit from our bodies in case this scenario came to pass.

South Koreans somewhat spoke like us. Strange and unexpected phrases and accents were audible to me. In the 1940s, time in North Korea was stunted, and as a result, so was the culture that served as a unifying force and the language that was used to communicate. It was like going through space and time to enter South Korea. High-speed trains, the internet, and casual clothing were all present—exactly as in the bootleg DVDs of South Korean operas.

While I was living in North Korea, I didn't put much effort into anything cerebral and was never a brilliant student. Everything changed when I was given the chance to earn a GED for both middle and high school in South Korea.

However, foreigners are not particularly welcome in South Korea's educational system. To begin with, with very few exceptions, all classes are taught in Korean, a challenging language with several cultural quirks and written in a distinct alphabet called Hangul. It's interesting that several subjects, including law and medicine, demand that Korean students learn English, but not so they can communicate; rather, it's so they can take in knowledge from English-language textbooks and the internet.

I could not keep up with the physical demands of training for the South Korean police force because of the starvation and poor health that followed me throughout my childhood in North Korea. I chose to pursue law school instead. I soon realized that I would also need to become fluent in English. I signed up for a rigorous tutoring course in Seoul that paired English-speaking foreign volunteers with North Korean defectors. I simultaneously signed up with ten tutors as opposed to only one! I studied under their guidance for eight months, learning about everyone from Shakespeare to the freed slave from America, Frederick Douglass.

I accepted other offers over the following few years, including one to represent North Korea at the One Young World summit in Ireland in 2014. This yearly event brings together student leaders from all across the world. The North Korean leadership provided three representatives in response to the OYW organization's request for just two. There was only enough space (or money) for two, but the regime wouldn't settle for anything less than three because it doesn't trust two people to be reliable spies. Two could plan to defect together. Three: A spies on B, B spies on C, and C spies on A, eliminates that risk. In the end, OYW declined and chose to invite defectors in its place. I received the call and flew to Dublin.

It was an especially heartfelt speech. James Chau, a well-known Chinese journalist who subsequently became a close friend, encouraged me to attend the event dressed in full traditional Korean garb—a flowing pink and white hanbok. James Chau also gave me an emotional introduction.

I suddenly felt a part of me starting to thaw. I had been made to conceal my feelings, harden my emotions, and train myself to become numb for a very long time. I made the decision to open my heart rather than read my prepared address as I got up on stage to make my brief speech in front of the 1,300 delegates, guests, and media representatives. That would be an American way of life.

Chapter 1:
Lost in the Big Apple

In November 2014, touching down in New York City was like landing on Mars. In 2013, I'd traveled on missions to Tyler, Texas, and Atlanta, Georgia. New York, though, was unique. It was not just a foreign country; it was a planet unto itself.

I had been granted the chance to write a book on my time in North Korea and my flight to China, so I was in New York. The nighttime views of the Manhattan towers from the taxi as we left John F. Kennedy International Airport, traveled along Grand Central Parkway, and across the Robert F. Kennedy Bridge were both majestic and ominous.

I had been alone in Seoul, confined to my home, my place of education, and the Now On My Way to Meet You set. I left South Korea with no more knowledge of how to move around in a contemporary city than I had when I had been a child in Hyesan. A sea of lights, steel, and glass awaited me as I emerged from a series of massive bridges and tunnels at the age of twenty-one.

Americans laugh when I describe what it was like for me because they only think of trash, crowds, tastelessness, weirdos, and tourists when they think of Times Square. However, for me, it was breathtaking. The North Korean leadership frequently claims that it would one day turn the United States into a "sea of fire" and that subsequent nuclear explosions will cause it to "glow in the dark." It appeared to be on fire already as I stood in the midst of Times Square. The enormous LED panels shone brighter at night than during the day thanks to the street and other people's faces. The lights danced rhythmically, at regular intervals, as if there were an invisible conductor tempting onlookers with apparel, a Broadway performance, fizzy water, or a pair of golden arches. It was a type of controlled pandemonium. (These were from Tyler and Seoul; it was something about a "happy meal.")

The only permanent structure in Hyesan was a statue of Kim Jong Il in the middle of the square that was lit up at night. It was typical to go without electricity for weeks or even months in other parts of the city. Candles were incredibly expensive, and flashlights with batteries were hard to come by. When I was younger, most of the games I played with my pals took place in the dark. And there I was, in the middle of a nighttime sea of light.

IT ALL started when my address at the One Young World conference in Dublin went viral. Later, I was requested to speak before the 30th United Nations Human Rights Council by the nonprofit UN Watch. I thought it was a fantastic honor, and I wanted to take the chance to raise awareness about how the Kim regime oppresses the people of North Korea. I was sitting quite near to the employees of the North Korean Permanent Mission to the United Nations for reasons that are still unknown, and they took advantage of the situation to intimidate and harass me with crude remarks.

Before the One Young World conference in 2014, I had the pleasure of meeting Thor Halvorssen, the organization's founder, at a "hackathon" they had organized in Silicon Valley to "hack North Korea." Even if I didn't fully comprehend what hacking was, I had enjoyed the experience and the lasting friendships I formed there. Later that year, I ran into another friend at the Oslo Freedom Forum (OFF) in Norway, where she told me of a program the US immigration system had to draw particular people to the country. I was curious, so I did some research and discovered the O-1 "Extraordinary" visa. Despite not knowing much about it, I chose to apply. Despite the little amount of time I spent there as a visitor, I never imagined myself relocating to Texas or Georgia.

The continuation of my studies was my first objective. In South Korea and throughout my travels, I had frequently heard that attending an American university would provide the best education possible. I was determined to enroll in a prestigious program and study under the best academics the nation has to offer. After some consideration, I decided to accept a scholarship offer to attend Columbia University, a prestigious school with a long list of prominent graduates that included Amelia Earhart, Warren Buffett, and the then-president of the United States, Barack Obama. In January 2016, I entered the revered grounds of Columbia University with complete elation.

I had to adjust to my new life as a North Korean in America before I could start my new life as a student there. In addition, many parts of New York life were the opposite of the only world I had ever known.

When Eunmi and I had to fend for ourselves during that year, we made a pact that if we ever grew up, we would earn as much money as we could so that we may consume bread till we were satisfied. We would disagree on how much food we believed we could consume. She claimed she could consume a whole bucket of bread; I asserted that I could consume five. I would say one hundred and she would say twenty. even a mountain of bread!

Seven thousand miles away, under the same sky, I was suddenly receiving information about "dietary restrictions." I went to see a friend in Brooklyn one evening, and he inquired about mine. I reacted, "I don't think I have any," The question "What are yours?" "Dairy, nuts, and gluten," she said. I enquired as to why out of curiosity. "Food allergies," she stated matter-of-factly. She was shocked when I inquired, "What are those?" She was gracious enough to educate me about people's moral limits, which I found more difficult to accept, as well as their physical restrictions after realizing the degree of my ignorance. It came out that there were a lot of people in New York who avoided eating any animal products, including non-meat alternatives.

One thing all of my early New York pals had in common was that they were all surprised by how much I ate. Large, juicy, grilled, healthy steak was my favorite food. It didn't matter if it was a tiny filet or a huge tomahawk. They had a certain magical quality. Cows have more rights than people in North Korea. Cows do not belong to ranchers; they belong to the government because private property rights do not exist. Only a select few members of the government are permitted to consume the meat, including numerous cattle ranchers who assist in raising and caring for them. My mother told me she once saw a young guy get put to death in the Hyesan market for killing a cow without getting permission from the authorities. Meat consumption wasn't only something I liked to do in New York. I had the impression that I was giving the North Korean government the middle finger with every bite.

Aside from physical health, Americans also appeared to have an intriguing perspective on mental health. The first thing my agency advised me to do was get a therapist to help me with my "trauma." I had no words for either idea in my native North Korean tongue, which was limited to adjectives and synonyms to depict a "socialist paradise" with "nothing to envy." As a result, I was unable to comprehend either idea. In North Korea, there are no words for oppression, trauma, depression, or even love. I found that it is simple enough to continue your life without even being aware of a feeling or phenomenon when there are no words to explain it. This truth is well understood by totalitarian governments.

Money was the other great surprise. As there is no financial system, private ownership, or markets in North Korea, many of the people I encountered in New York worked in the banking industry. The one financial lesson my father ever gave me was to never, ever take on debt. Despite the fact that most private ownership and financial activities are prohibited in North Korea, there are many "private lenders" that make a lot of money by making loans with a monthly fee.

My parents occasionally took out loans from these loan sharks to keep their business afloat, but when the black market prices fell and a lot of their goods were seized or stolen, they were unable to repay the money they had borrowed, which was less than two dollars in value. Every evening as we ate our meager meal, debt collectors would arrive at the house. In front of my sister and I, they frequently cursed and threatened my parents. My father finally felt he had had enough at a certain time. This was the decision that signaled the beginning of the end for us in North Korea when he decided to enter the considerably riskier business of smuggling precious metals like copper, nickel, and cobalt into China. One day, he advised me, "Yeonmi-ya, never borrow money, no matter how difficult life becomes. Having debt might diminish your sense of dignity.

THEN came racial issues. We learn that we are members of the Kim Il Sung Race in North Korea. I was unaware that I was Asian when I was a child. I was unaware of what Asia was. I was merely one of many millions of a single man's offspring.

I encountered Jewish Americans, European Americans, Asian Americans, Arab Americans, and African Americans in New York. I had no idea about the many racial and cultural prejudices attached to each group's members, and I had no concept of the subtle differences between various ethnic groups or the historical reasons for each one's existence. In retrospect, it was a fascinating social science experiment. What would happen if you dropped a twenty-one-year-old white-bread candidate, to whom all notions of race and racism are wholly new, in New York City?

From where I was standing, America appeared to be the melting pot of myth, with all various kinds of people coexisting, mingling, falling in love with one another, and simply existing. It was lovely! But this was only going to be the start of a protracted and challenging lesson, which I go into more detail about in later chapters.

In America, I observed that sidewalks were reduced to provide a place for wheelchair users, that every building had both stairs and elevators, and that everything from public restrooms to public transit had special accessibility features. Later, I discovered that this was a result of the 1990 Americans with Disabilities Act, which Congress passed.

Accommodations for individuals with disabilities, a single, constrained aspect of life, came to stand for everything I was coming to love about America: democracy, self-determination, civic engagement, entrepreneurship, solidarity, and compassion.

Chapter 2:
The Fall of Lady Columbia

One of the few American institutions that predates the nation itself is Columbia. It was founded in 1754, twenty-two years before the Declaration of Independence and thirty-three years before the Constitution. It was first known as King's College and was located on the grounds of Trinity Church. It was founded by royal charter during the reign of King George II. I quickly discovered that the name change took place in 1784, following the American Revolutionary War. The university's name was changed to Columbia thanks in large part to Alexander Hamilton and John Jay, who were at the time trustees on the university's board of trustees. The common misconception that "pertaining to Christopher Columbus" is all that the word "Columbia" denotes is at best inaccurate.

The feminine counterpart of Uncle Sam, Lady Columbia is a national personification of the United States of America. A stunning young woman extending outstretched arms or a blazing torch, illuminating the path to the promised land, is the classic representation. Typically, paintings show a severe visage with a knowing smile. She is an American Mona Lisa who exudes both assurance and comfort.

In revolutionary art, the image of a stunning lady lifting her arm in defiance is commonplace. One of the most enduring representations of the French Republic is Marianne or Liberty lifting the flag and leading soldiers over the barricades, which is one of the most famous images of the French Revolution. Both the Bolsheviks and the anti-Bolshevik White faction referred to Russia as "Mother Russia" during the Russian Civil War. Immigrants to America have anxiously awaited the chance to see a tarnished copper statue of the clad goddess of liberty looming in Upper New York Bay for 137 years.

Wheatley, who was born in West Africa in 1753 and bought as a slave in Boston, went on to create the first collection of poetry ever written by an African American, earning her fame in both London and the American colonies. After three of her children died, she was finally set free by her captors thanks to the publishing of her book, but she died a forgotten and impoverished woman at age 31.

Such tales abound in American history, depicting lives that are rife with conflict: anguish and victory, oppression and emancipation, failure and success, evil and good, all of which coexist side by side, simultaneously, as they do in every human heart. It is a testament to the genius of America that a West African slave's literary aptitude and brilliance was ever discovered; it is a tragedy of America that she was destroyed by the conditions to which she was subjected. Without acknowledging these realities, it is difficult to comprehend American history or the nature of the American people—a reality that Columbia University, to my surprise, would make every effort to hide.

Masterpieces of Western Music was one of the key classes I was most eager to take. I had found Beethoven and Chopin in South Korea, and my favorite pieces were the piano sonatas. I had a sensation of transcendence when listening to Beethoven's music in particular, as have millions of other listeners throughout the world for the past 200 years. I had read that Beethoven served as a bridge between Western music's Classical and Romantic eras, and I was curious as to what it meant when music without lyrics was referred to as "romantic." Naturally, the state in North Korea has worked to eradicate the very idea of romance, as the only kind of love it condones is the one between the people and their Dear Leader. I'd largely learned about romance between couples through piracy in movies and television shows, but in music? I was eager to discover.

My lack of knowledge related to "the nuances and subtleties of gender interactions in a new culture: in academia." And since none of them are natural or evident, they must all be learned. The lecturer questioned me about how I came to know that I couldn't lift as many bricks as a man could. I simply stated that I was eighty pounds, which I was.

In the four years I wound up spending at Columbia, humanities professors constantly pushed us to show how awake we were. In order to be truly awakened, we had to work hard to identify the white male Bastards who were responsible for every crime, every issue, and even the air we breathed. If we didn't, we were just as bad as those who actively support social injustice. Luckily, it was a simple job for the open-minded kids. The inquiries were always foreseen, and the responses were always manufactured. Students weren't asked to discuss the content; only to regurgitate what had been said. Not to think or comprehend, but simply memorize and recite. It was passion and intensity that made the difference between a passing grade and a spectacular one, not accuracy or creativity. Refusing to critique the standard targets (capitalism, Western culture, white supremacy, systemic racism, persecution of minorities, colonialism, etc.) is what made the difference between a passing grade and a failing one. Being called a "SIX HIRB"—a bigot who is sexist, intolerant, xenophobic, homophobic, Islamophobic, and racist—by one's peers was worse than receiving a poor score.

I clearly remember a teacher asking us to answer the equation $1 + 1$ when I was a very young student in North Korea. I've always struggled in school, but when I finally knew the answer to a question, "Two!" I exclaimed with pride. "Wrong," the teacher replied. She continued by elaborating on one of our Dear Leader's greatest lessons. Like us, Kim Jong Il made the discovery that mathematics was made up when he was a young child, making him the first person in history to do so. He said that when two drops of water are combined, they form one large drop rather than two smaller ones.

The distressing insight of the Dear Leader has two points. The first is to begin teaching young children to accept something so blatantly stupid and incorrect as a fact. (You can frighten her into quitting talking about it, but not even a child can be convinced that the sum of two sticks is just a large stick.) The second is to show kids that they are not unique beings. One person plus one person does not equal two individuals, and a society is not made up of 21 million people. The only number in North Korea is one—one leader, followed by one person.

It was difficult to avoid thinking about how Christians and people of all faiths are persecuted in North Korea, where communist fundamentalism views religion as the "opiate of the masses" (to use

Karl Marx's terminology), and where the Kim family has appropriated the central Christian tenet for its own particular political agenda: Kim Il Sung is God, the father, who gave us his son Kim Jong Il, the Christ.

To put it mildly, everything was turning out to be a fairly unpleasant experience. How could one of the best universities in the biggest nation on earth educate its students to despise their compatriots? What is the purpose of this damaging narrative? Isn't the goal of an American institution to educate thoughtful, courteous people who can engage in productive conversation and social interaction?

This was going to be a long four years, that much was evident.

Chapter 3:
The Illusion of Safe Space

The modern classroom is a holdover from a time when education was primarily intended to educate children and teenagers for adult life in an industrial society. dozens of frequently uneducated pupils sat at similar desks, spaced evenly apart, and looking in the same direction so as to receive daily teaching from the same teacher at the same times: Early in the 20th century, this completely unnatural arrangement made sense since young people genuinely needed to be prepared for entry into a mass, commercial society as well as for positions in factories or as secretaries.

By upholding the wide educational ideals of the Enlightenment, the issue has usually been avoided in the West. Critical thinking was reintroduced into elementary schools and universities during the turbulent eighteenth-century Enlightenment. As the Socratic technique of instructing by asking questions and learning by combining various responses from various people was already thousands of years old, this was in fact a reintroduction rather than an invention. Muslim scholars carried Socratic education into the dark ages of dogma and superstition when Europe fell into them. However, the West would finally see a renaissance.

ASIDE After the Jane Austen episode, I experienced another significant moment at Columbia orientation. Faculty and administrators went around the room and briefed us on Columbia's body of policies—the student Code of Conduct—in the interest of assisting incoming students "assimilate" to life at the university. The school advertises that it turns out thinkers who are well-rounded, but that wasn't the case here. Maintaining the classroom as a "safe space" was the only objective that was given laser-like concentration.

I was perplexed. The Columbia University campus, dorms, and related buildings and residential apartments struck me as eminently safe, and Morningside Heights as a wonderfully nice area. I was aware that New York City had a history of violent crime. Although the word "literal" was wrongly used multiple times, I immediately understood that the teachers' use of the word "safe" did not refer to literal physical safety but rather to everyone's apparent right to refrain from experiencing emotional or psychological harm. Several professors made reference to the potential for emotional injury in order to obliquely explain—in so many words—why Socratic technique is prohibited in Columbia courses.

Even though it was funny, I was quite worried that I would end up getting kicked out of school for endangering the safety of a fellow student. The Code did little to clarify the phrases, which made them look incredibly ambiguous. How could I predict who would be disturbed by what if any word or action may make someone else uncomfortable, and if discomfort was a reason for potential disciplinary action? I had no idea who anyone was or what they thought.

AS A NEWBORN Things became crazier as the year went on, I took more classes, and I advanced in my knowledge. One time a professor warned students in an email that they wouldn't be expected to finish reading assignments if a particular element of the assignment brought up unpleasant memories or sentiments. The email continued, "Don't even come to class, and don't feel obligated to explain why you were triggered." Emotional support animals were now permitted on campus and even encouraged inside of classrooms, according to the new policy. During one lesson, I recall someone's dog licking my shoes, and I was at a loss for words other than to chuckle.

Of course, in actuality, Columbia's "safe space" was simply elitist jargon for restrictions on intellectual diversity. I had pictured Columbia as a marketplace of ideas, where students had limitless opportunities to challenge conventional wisdom and forge on toward a better future. In this sense, a "safe space" would probably refer to a location where opinions might be voiced without concern for retaliation. Instead, it referred to a setting where—to flip the expression made famous by Ben Shapiro—emotions don't care about your facts. I started to lose hope that my new institutional home would serve as a cult rather than a means of seeking the truth.

My South Korean tutors, however, didn't get the memo and appeared to be extremely outdated, using English grammatical standards that were only in use from roughly 1450 to 2014: In actuality, there are 78 gender pronouns. Some, like Zie/Ze, reminded me of Americans doing poor German impressions—an odd preference—while others, like Ver/Vis, brought to mind Latin class tongue twisters. My particular favorites were Xe/Xem and Xyr, which resembled elements from Mendeleev's periodic table both visually and sonically. The majority have nothing in common with other English words. I was finding it difficult to learn my new language and was feeling really insecure about it. No matter how hard I tried to remember their pronouns, I now risked the danger of insulting my friends by using the wrong pronouns. As if these relationships weren't complex enough, it was impossible to even guess at these pronouns by looking at the morphological characteristics of my classmates.

I really do mean it when I say that I had nothing but compassion, empathy, and understanding for this guy. They were just very recent immigrants who made a mistake that, in accordance with what I had been taught, wasn't actually a mistake, so I couldn't blame them for feeling entitled to speak to me as if I were a bigot. This person had no idea what justice or injustice meant or looked like; they were simply lost and entirely disconnected from life. Furthermore, they were probably not at fault.

Years later, in 2019, I decided to speak about this subject when I gave a TED Talk in Vancouver. Many people believe that individuals are intrinsically aware of fairness and injustice and that we are all born with strong moral convictions that enable us to recognize right from wrong. This, in my opinion, is rubbish.

Because of what I was taught from an early age, I was brainwashed to think that the Kims were starving much like us when I lived in North Korea. I didn't realize Kim Jong Il couldn't possible be starving until a friend in South Korea pointed out to me that he had a big, round belly. In other words, even if a baby might have observed that Kim Jong Il was overweight, I had to be trained to apply logic to determine this.

I have grown to appreciate the world's unfathomable complexity throughout the course of my twenty-nine years here. In fact, it is referred to by the acronym VUCA, which stands for volatility, uncertainty, complexity, and ambiguity, in the U.S. military. VUCA stands for all elements that cause human uncertainty and disquiet and was first used to define the post-Cold War environment. The complexity and uncertainty of daily life, particularly in the current day, are so great that most people can neither begin to comprehend it nor even want to try—it is simply too overwhelming.

"In Lumine Tuo Videbimus Lumen" is the Latin phrase that serves as Columbia University's motto; it is taken from Psalms (36:9) and means "In Thy light shall we see light." However, neither in the world nor in people did the Columbia I knew see any light. It only perceived the dark, which I knew to be a falsehood.

Chapter 4:
Hypocrisy of the Elite

The Rise of the Meritocracy, penned by British sociologist and politician Michael Young in 1958, has since become a classic. Young's satire, written in response to the postwar tripartite public education system, depicted a dystopian United Kingdom where "merit" replaced class as the main source of division, creating a society with a strong elite on the one hand and a weak underclass on the other. Instead of being a prediction of a class of educated, technical elites who gain power and use it at the expense of regular people who can never aspire to reach their ranks, the book is sometimes misinterpreted as a critique of merit.

I still attended the Oslo Freedom Forum in October 2014 when I got an invitation from an organization called Amazon from a man by the name of Jeff Bezos. I responded that I would be busy (even though I wasn't!) because I had never heard of either. Several conferences, including Women in the World, which was organized by Tina Brown, the original editor-in-chief of the Daily Beast, requested me to speak. I was slated to speak at Women in the World before Hillary Rodham Clinton, whose name I was familiar with from news reports about South Korea while she served as secretary of state. prominent speakers at the event were Jon Stewart from The Daily Show, Meryl Streep, a well-known actress, and prominent politicians like Samantha Power, who was serving as the United States' ambassador to the UN at the time.

This conference marked a turning point in my life and how I saw the world. Up until that moment, I had assumed that the lack of action on the part of the international community was due to ignorance of the situation in North Korea. After all, no one in North Korea can connect with the outside world, and just approximately 200 North Korean defectors have legitimately entered America in the past more than seventy years. When I agreed to speak at the conference, I made a commitment to take advantage of the chance to inform the distinguished audience about the reality of the situation in North Korea in the hopes that it would motivate and inspire Americans and

Europeans with true wealth, influence, and ability to take action. I was confident that they would at the very least assist in disseminating information about the contemporary holocaust occurring in North Korea, about how the Chinese Communist Party is aiding and abetting it, and about how tens of thousands, perhaps even hundreds of thousands, of mostly female North Korean defectors are being sold, raped, and otherwise harmed in China.

That wasn't what happened, to put it simply. It turned out that the point of a conference like Women in the World was to passionately discuss the suffering of women in America, not to mobilize the financial and political power of those who are fortunate enough to have it to help people suffering in places like China and North Korea. The term "oppression" in this context was interpreted to include factors like earning just 90 cents on the dollar compared to males, serving as the vice president rather than the CEO of a Fortune 500 business, or how a male-dominated workplace environment prevents women from crying in public. I once more struggled to trust what I was hearing despite my best efforts to be kind.

Hillary Clinton was the speaker after me, so she listened to my speech from the green room backstage. She was running for president at the time, in October of 2015. She had on a black-and-white jacket that, in my memory, made her look somewhat like Kim Jong Il's signature winter coat while also making her resemble former German chancellor Angela Merkel. After my address, as I was leaving the platform in tears, Clinton approached me, looked me in the eye, and promised to never forget what I had said. She pledged to do all in her power to assist the North Korean women.

If she had been elected president, she might have, but I doubt it. But after her political aspirations were dashed the following year, she decided to spend the next few years (as far as I could tell) whining about not being president instead of using her considerable personal fame and power to manage the enormous funds of the nonprofit Clinton Foundation. Since then, she has never brought up the horrors experienced by North Korean women. None at all.

I can still clearly recall my fiancé calling to inform me that Trump had won. I was terrified and lying in bed. I started crying. When I called my pals to check on them, they also called to see how I was doing. I spent the entire day reading the major national newspapers, listening to the radio, and watching cable news. It was obvious that Trump had worked with the Russians to steal the election from Clinton and that he would soon be impeached, if not killed. If not, then America, where I had gone in quest of freedom, would soon experience the black night of fascism. It was just bad luck that I'd finally gotten here in time to see it collapse into the dictatorship I'd fled from.

I suddenly lived in a world where the Republic, peace, and freedom might all be lost with the win of a single election for one of America's two major political parties. This was the elite world, the world of the New York Times, the Washington Post, NPR, and Columbia.

I did not finally kick this habit thanks to the education I got at Columbia or from reading the American press. Reading old books was involved. The Rise of the Meritocracy by Michael Young and George Orwell's collected works are two examples. I came to believe—and still do—that the best way to think for yourself is to tune out the major media, essentially forget the daily news cycle, and connect with the great thinkers of the past who understand all of our problems better than we do. They have a better understanding of them than we do. The great works of Western culture are all prohibited in autocracies for a reason.

I was given another speaking invitation in March 2016—this time to a gathering dubbed "Campfire." A select group of well-known and successful writers, artists, musicians, and filmmakers gather once or twice a year for an exclusive, off-the-record weekend of relaxation, socializing, and storytelling by fascinating people who have lived extraordinary lives. By this time, I knew Jeff Bezos was the founder and CEO of Amazon and that this was a very large company. Previous visitors have included Billie Jean King, Walter Mosley, Tom Hanks, Neil Gaiman, Robert Sapolsky, Neil Armstrong, Bette Midler, and Ron Howard, in no particular sequence. The event that year would take place at the Biltmore Hotel in Santa Barbara, California, from September 29 to October 2. visitors were requested to write 25-minute presentations that they would deliver to 150 other distinguished visitors.

I took the week off from my academics and continued my human rights advocacy activities at the time to attend Campfire. Several participants, including myself, were picked up in New York by a Gulfstream private plane sent by Bezos. I remember one of the passengers who identified himself as Harvey Weinstein, but I can't recall the names of the other prominent actors and authors who were on the plane with me. My fiance informed me that he was a well-known film producer even though I had no idea who he was.

Naturally, this was my first time flying in a private jet, and I had never seen a more stunning aircraft. We took off from a private airport, so there was no security or baggage check. I had just left a morning session at Columbia on a sunny but cool day. By this point, I had heard more about Jeff Bezos, who was now apparent to be one of the richest and most powerful persons on the planet in addition to being the CEO of Amazon. I was confident that with his assistance, I would be able to find a way to improve the lot of North Koreans—if not the ones trapped in the country itself, then at least some of the 300,000 defectors in China, where I'd heard Bezos did a lot of his business. I boarded his plane with the same optimism I had when I took the stage at the Women in the World conference. It wouldn't take much, in my opinion; just someone like Bezos acknowledging what was happening to my people in China might start a chain reaction that persuaded other American investors to put pressure on Beijing to stop supporting Pyongyang.

We ate a lot of food on the flight. There was an abundance of food and endless beverages. Before I was too ashamed to ask for more food, I must have eaten 10 plates, so I assigned my fiance to make several visits to the buffet on his own to bring me refills. The Gulfstream traveled far more quickly than the typical commercial aircraft, and the loud engine noise injured my ears. My fiance casually inquired about the cost of chartering one of these

Gulfstreams for the brief time it required to travel across the nation. They claimed it cost more than $100,000!

I had begun to have some whiplash from my new life in 2016, and now I was really beginning to feel it. My mother and I were bought and sold in China for $65 for her and less than $300 for me. Looking down on the planet where we were bought for sex and sold into slavery just a few thousand kilometers away, I was soaring over the same blue sky, illuminated by the same sun. And here I was, soaring through the air for a sum that, along with that of hundreds, if not thousands, of other North Korean women and girls in China, might have instantly purchased our freedom. And we were en route to a conference where we were meant to motivate one another to live extraordinary lives! People with extra money could, if they wished, figuratively buy the freedom of their fellow humans; no think group, foundation, or NGO is required to figure out how to aid people. However, there we were at a buffet traveling at 600 mph while 30,000 feet in the air, setting that money ablaze as we got ready to discuss how to "do good" in the world.

I've dealt with survivor's guilt for a long time, which is described by the American Psychological Association as "remorse or guilt for having survived a catastrophic event when others did not." Even now, I frequently dream about the loved ones I left behind in North Korea as well as those who have endured hardship because of their proximity to or previous connections to me during the years since I became somewhat famous. My mother and I employed middlemen in China and North Korea to wire money to family members after we defected. In the years that followed, we discovered that those brokers were no longer able to find our ancestors. They were probably killed, abducted, or imprisoned.

I've discovered that the only way to maintain mental stability is to make every effort to find significance in my good fortune and the things I've decided to accomplish with it. I am aware of how fortunate I am and that I did not work for my freedom. I'm not smarter or more resilient than other people who have battled for their freedom and failed. I occasionally think of it as pure luck. In other cases, I have the impression that someone from above handed me this hand and doesn't just want me to enjoy it. He anticipates that I would share my blessings in addition to counting them.

Harvey Weinstein spoke to the audience on the first day of the conference about his life, describing how he started out with nothing and how, after becoming so improbable wealthy, he now gives back by aiding those who are less fortunate. His comments moved me to tears. Despite not coming from a wealthy family or having any connections to key figures, he persevered and worked hard to rise to the top of one of the most important and culturally significant sectors in America, if not the entire world. As I listened to him talk, I realized that, at least in terms of context, his experience and mine weren't all that dissimilar. America, the land of opportunity, where anyone willing to work hard and endure could succeed, even a nobody from Flushing, Queens, the son of Polish immigrants, or even a desperately destitute refugee from North Korea, who scarcely knew English, made it possible for his tale to be told.

Everyone enthusiastically applauded and hooted on this sunny California morning in the fall of 2016, when Clinton's victory was all but certain and Weinstein was nothing more than a genius who had made the dreams of young actresses come true. Later that day, they delighted in reminiscing about their pleasant surprise at what a hero Weinstein was. When I watched how the other Campfire participants treated him at lunch—waiting in line to greet him, shaking his hand, embracing and kissing him reverently—I started to think of him almost as a saint. After all, I had thought highly of him after his lecture.

In less than a year, he had been credibly accused of perpetrating sex offenses over a forty-year period by eighty women. Some of the attendees at Campfire, including one well-known actress, would go on to play major roles in the #MeToo campaign, whose eventual spokesperson ended up being Weinstein. When I asked one of the people I had met at Campfire if she was aware of Weinstein's actions before they were made public, she said that of course she was—everyone was. I didn't?

The opportunity to speak came up the next morning. The issue that dominated Campfire, but on which I didn't plan to speak, was the threat to American democracy faced by Trump's nomination. I was preceded by virtual remarks from well-known political personalities, including Georgia representative John Lewis.

I stepped up to the podium and began by apologizing to Jeff Bezos, who was sitting in the front row with his wife and young children. I made an effort to establish some rapport by saying that the only reason I had declined his earlier offer was because I didn't know who he was. I also admitted that, with the exception of Tom Hanks and Reese Witherspoon, I still didn't know who most of the people in the audience were. Everyone laughed, though a little more awkwardly than I'd expected, as if I were a guest from Saturn rather than an immigrant from another nation.

I said that the only reason I was in front of them that morning was because of my father's straightforward lesson since, for me, choosing to live has always been the most difficult option.

After my speech, it finally happened: a few politicians, businesses, and actors approached me and inquired as to how they may be of assistance. The single most effective thing they could do was to raise awareness about the Communist Party's sponsorship of the contemporary Holocaust in North Korea and the modern-day slave trade of North Koreans in China. I told them how much it would cost to buy the freedom of an enslaved North Korean girl in China, but that China has a very sophisticated and impenetrable system of human trafficking.

Early in 2017, I received an invitation from one of Airbnb's founders to the Met Gala, a yearly ball that raises money for the Metropolitan Museum of Art's New York City fashion display. The gala that year had the theme "Edge," and a stylist was sent in who bought clothing from Australian museums. I was unaware of the magnitude of the occasion and still didn't recognize most of the attendees. My belief in events like this had all but vanished, and it was obvious that the event was superficial and pointless, but I reasoned that it was still worth a shot in case I met just one person who would be interested in and had the resources to accept my advocacy at face value.

Wendi Deng Murdoch, Rupert's ex-wife, and a few other billionaires who owned some of the greatest IT businesses in the world were seated next to me for a portion of the evening. They discussed Swiss-made diamonds, their favorite supermodels, and—get ready for this shocking one—how much they detested Donald Trump. They asked me not to mention them in any of my speeches or in any public forum owing to their connections to China when I sheepishly ventured to introduce myself at one point during the evening and inquired why on earth I'd been invited to attend this event with them.

I gave talks about what I understood was going on under the Chinese Communist Party and the North Korean government at Google, Facebook, the United Nations, the U.S. Department of State, and the TED conference throughout the course of the ensuing years. Everywhere I went, the same sequence of things happened: lots of crying, lots of hugging and shaking hands, plenty of solicitous empathy and offers of assistance, all followed by lots of silence.

Later, I learned that these elites made "Silence is violence" their go-to political and cultural catchphrase. Many of them I saw again over the following four years, this time on my TV, protesting against Trump in pink, police in black, climate change in green, and other colors, and railing against the system that had allowed them to become some of the most privileged people in history.

Over the course of the following four years, many of the people who seemed to be listening intently when I explained what they could do to change the world instead spent their time constantly warning the country about fascists in the White House, Russian puppets in the Oval Office, and white nationalists holding infants in cages. In response to an existential threat—a president they didn't vote for—they lobbied against the impartial application of laws and truth in the media, which they no longer considered as democratic principles.

When I told them about my life and job, I began to worry if they had the same impression of me. Oh, poor little Asian kid, she's too gullible and innocent to see that the issue isn't China's or North Korea's oppressive regimes. In America, there is a dictatorship and slavery.

Permit me to share one more story, which is noteworthy since it was the first time I saw overt corruption in America.

One of these "off-the-record" private dinners was to be held by Tina Brown of Women in the World and the Daily Beast. I was invited one day. In late September of 2019 at the five-star St. Regis Hotel in New York during the United Nations General Assembly, Tina co-hosted a private event with Brian Moynihan, the CEO of Bank of America. Imran Khan, the leader of Pakistan, and Nancy Pelosi, the speaker of the House, were also invited. Tycoons from the media, fashion, Hollywood, technology, banking, and academic sectors were also represented. I recall a renowned Chinese venture capitalist sitting next to a New York Times journalist.

I understood the message: The market would decline when the news of the impeachment was announced. Only one night remains for you to shorten it. The Washington Post announced the impeachment inquiry the following day, and the market dropped as expected.

A few weeks later, Pelosi stated, "If we allow one president—any president, no matter who she or he may be—to go down this path, we are saying goodbye to the republic and hello to a president-king."

Chapter 5:
Values in Decline

The devotion of the United States of America to each person's inalienable rights to life, liberty, and the pursuit of happiness is what I admire most about it, both in theory and in practice. It's challenging to explain to native-born Americans how unique that last right is as a value, let alone one upheld by the government. The majority of nations are either dedicated to something ruthlessly practical, like their own security or survival, or to abstract concepts like the "glory," "majesty," or "destiny" of a people or government. However, America is committed to ensuring that every citizen has the freedom to pursue happiness. Of course, this does not ensure that anyone in particular will be content. However, America was built on the principle that no one, no group, and no institution has the right to restrict another person's ability to pursue happiness. The Declaration of Independence, the text that codifies this principle, is written in exquisite language to reflect this completely wonderful vision, and it makes me proud to be human as well as an American.

It became more difficult for me to ignore what the "right to pursue happiness" meant to many Americans of my generation as I drew closer to my mid-20s. The oozing vanity of the fashion and nightlife industries, the insatiable greed of the financial world, and the envy of power and material gain that seemed to make everyone I knew almost hopelessly envious of others and unhappy with their own lives seemed to flourish in particular in New York City and be elevated as a virtue in themselves.

Many of my companions in New York had the bad habit of intentionally going out on many weekends for one-night hookups, which only appeared to make them feel more regretful and alone. I had never heard of the idea of a mobile dating app until one of them showed it to me, so I assumed it was a joke and that all the men on it were false. Particularly several of my more senior friends—married ones too—encouraged me to spend these years—my early twenties—dating around without settling down. They were particularly fond of using metaphors related to the ocean, such as "test the waters," "dip your toe," and "there are so many fish in the sea," which I still have difficulties understanding.

But for a while, the novelty of it all amused me. For me, the idea of being free to love whomever you want has never lost its potency. The rigorous caste system known as songbun in North Korea forbids marrying or even amicable interaction between various classes, which is intended to limit opportunities for social mobility. If a person from a lower caste marries someone from a higher caste, the higher caste person is always degraded to the lower caste—never the other way around. Naturally, this discourages people from mingling and "marrying down." Such is socialism's classless paradise: In North Korea, most weddings are planned between families or mandated by the state. As a result of more young people being exposed to stolen South Korean television dramas, the idea of dating has gradually filtered down to the younger strata of society. The young, however, continue to be cautious about taking any action that could lower their family's status when it comes to marriage.

But in America, no one appeared to mind that I had a thick East Asian accent and spoke severely broken English. I received a warm welcome and experienced true acceptance for the first time in my life. I was delighted to discover that Dr. King's dream—that nearly all Americans appeared ready to evaluate me not by the color of my skin, but by the content of my character—was a reality. People were understanding and sympathetic. Because of that, it was fascinating to think of finding a loving partner. It would be as if I had the entire world at my disposal if everyone here had the freedom to date whoever they wanted without discrimination and New York was a melting pot of races, ethnicities, and religions. Not only would I not be limited to dating and eventually marrying a man from Korea and from my own low caste, but I would also have the opportunity to experience true love. As a matter of fact, my first relationship in America was with a Jewish man whose family had fled the Soviet Union when he was eight years old; despite our various racial, religious, and socioeconomic origins, this relationship was successful.

Particularly in New York City, the majority of the males I encountered were a little mysterious to me. "Dating material" and "marriage material" are not applicable terms (or terms that even exist) in North Korea. People go on dates to get married, and they get married to start a family. Although dating might be thrilling, it's still a somewhat sober and respectable procedure. But in New York, it appeared like people dated largely to get wasted and have sex. Sometimes on Sunday mornings, my girlfriends would call or text me to express their disappointment that the guy they went out and had sex with the night before had disappeared, or even that their long-term boyfriends had ended things when the subject of engagement or even just exclusivity came up.

In North Korea, a man's duty to a woman is to protect and take care of her. Perhaps that gender dynamic is far too constricting and rigid, but I began to understand that I at least preferred it to the contemporary Western dynamic, where males are allegedly pushed to feel absolutely no responsibility for the women they woo.

No one seemed to pause and consider whether they might be personally to blame for their own unhappiness in the midst of the arguments that gender is a construct, complaining about "toxic masculinity" and "mansplaining," declaring that the idea of a "protector" or "provider" is sexist, that marriage is archaic, and that children rob you of your freedom.

From that point forward, anytime a man I was interested in asked me out, I informed him that I only dated men exclusively and that my ultimate goal was marriage. Of course, my girlfriends told me not to say things like that since they would scare the hell out of any rational young man and make him run the other way. However, I just reasoned that any man who would be afraid of commitment would likely also be afraid to be responsible or loving, making him unworthy of my attention. In any case, I had no fear of being single, which, in my opinion, was far preferable to being in a relationship with the wrong person or for the wrong reasons.

Fortunately, my first relationship was with a gentleman. He was very responsible and honest. Additionally, it was the first time I had ever experienced love feelings. Though initially difficult, I was glad to have met someone who possessed many of my ideals. Insecure about myself and my surroundings at the age of twenty-one and still relatively new to America, I eventually gave in to peer pressure. I ended our relationship after a year of dating because I thought I was being unfaithful by not "testing the waters" and getting to know the "other fish in the sea." But I soon understood that I wasn't at all happy doing this kind of activity.

Then, during a friend's birthday celebration in the sweltering summer of 2016, I met a very peculiar "American Bastard." He had studied books, seen documentaries, and took an interest in North Korea, which he knew quite a bit about. He appeared to sincerely care about the suffering of the people there. He also held the same beliefs I did about the value of family. We fell in love right away, and by the time we got married in downtown Manhattan in late 2016, I was 23 and he was 32. The Statue of Liberty could be seen in the distance from the location where we did the ceremony. That day, I recall thinking that my experience could only happen in America.

International unions are not permitted in North Korea. If an unborn child is not "pureblood," they are frequently killed and pregnant women are compelled to get abortions. Sometimes, women who flee to China only to be raped become pregnant. If discovered and returned to North Korea, the government will utilize cruel means to forcefully terminate the pregnancy. They will continuously kick pregnant women's tummies, inject them with saltwater using needles, or put a big wooden board on their bellies and make small children jump on it. In certain cases, the government will place the helpless infant in a box and leave it to perish if, by some miracle, the child is born nonetheless.

I couldn't believe how far I had gone from that nightmare—marrying an American on Manhattan Island in front of Lady Liberty. How I adored every second of my new life and the entirety of this new nation, flaws and all, and how sincerely appreciative I was to have the freedom to follow my heart wherever it may lead.

The strongest connection between my husband and I was our mutual desire for purpose and fulfilling lives. I was fully aware of the difficulties life may present when lacking purpose. In his classic, Man's Search for Meaning, the famous psychiatrist and Holocaust survivor Viktor E. Frankl writes, "If you find a why, then you can bear any how." My husband and I were dedicated to our "why," which was foremost to start a family.

We attempted to get pregnant not long after getting married. However, because I was chronically undernourished for the first fourteen years of my life, I was and continue to be exceedingly underweight. Despite being five feet two inches tall, I weighed less than eighty pounds even in 2016. We eventually came to the conclusion that my childhood trauma and starvation would prevent me from becoming pregnant naturally. Our choice was to proceed with in vitro fertilization (IVF). How amazing, I recall thinking, that I now had the chance to use this great technology in order to realize my motherhood dream, when my hometown of Hyesan doesn't even have dependable electricity.

I visited the infertility clinic in the early hours of numerous mornings to have my blood drawn and to see if I was pregnant. I recall seeing a lot of women there who were clearly very intelligent and ambitious and were just as eager to get pregnant as I was. Even though it was terrible to see so many women struggling, it was actually encouraging to see all these accomplished and powerful women working so hard to have children. In the summer of 2017, I finally became pregnant after numerous injections, trials, and the third IVF attempt.

One of my happiest days in life was the day I learned. In actuality, my sister-in-law and I were en route to the New York Gay Pride Parade when I learned the test's results. The emotion of extreme thankfulness for the miracle process that had started inside of me was the one I recall feeling the most that day.

I regularly had sonograms throughout my pregnancy, and my doctor recommended that I take prenatal vitamins and iron supplements. I recall thinking at the time that all the hardships I had previously experienced had been worthwhile since it meant that my child would have a fantastic existence here in America, beginning even with the vitamins I would be able to give them while they were still in the womb.

You can therefore imagine my thoughts at this point on the never-ending and increasingly shrill stream of discussions, debates, and news reports about the fascist hellhole that America has evolved into.

I left Columbia for a semester and relocated to Chicago, where my husband's firm was based, to give birth to our kid. Early in 2018, I was rather overwhelmed to learn about all the things you're required to buy, have, and know in order to care for an American baby, just like many other American mothers. I had no idea about swings, cribs, bathtubs, disposable diapers, non-disposable diapers, wipes, pumps, bibs, formula, bottles, bottle warmers, bottle sterilizers, bottle warmers, disposable diapers, non-disposable diapers, wipes, pumps, or bibs, much alone terms like "sleep training" and "self-led weaning."

Evidently, North Korea has very little of this. The infant will starve to death in North Korea if the mother is unable to produce breast milk and there is no available wet nurse. This is frequently the case since many North Korean mothers are unable to lactate due to severe and pervasive malnutrition. This contrasts sharply with parenting in America, where parents purchase items like the "Frida," which makes it possible to remove snot from a baby's nose, and the "Windi," which relieves flatulence.

My appreciation for the Americans who came before me and created this just and successful country has grown as I have settled in the beautiful Midwest. I couldn't help but marvel at the wonders of the free market and the entrepreneurialism that went into the medical care, child care, and parenting products that American parents were expected to take advantage of, and to which even Americans of limited means still had some degree of access, despite how overwhelming it was to prepare for childbirth.

The happiest day of my life was the day my son was born. Nothing else in the world mattered to me in those early days, and it still doesn't.

I had a cesarean section on the day of delivery since my body wasn't big enough to support a healthy natural birth. I couldn't believe how lucky I was to be his mother when the doctors took him out of my womb and laid him on my chest so I could hold him in my arms and stroke his skin with my cheeks. He was such a wonderful little baby, and I just couldn't fathom how I could possibly deserve to be his mother. I recalled at the time contemplating my distant foremothers and seeing all the ladies who had endured hardships like starvation, war, famine, and wilderness to give birth and sustain life in order that one day I would do the same in a hospital, in peace and health.

I finally understood what happiness was at that point. It is merely a term for affection and appreciation. Happiness is not achievement in the financial world, acclaim, or even comfort. It involves having children, being a good daughter, a good friend, and providing assistance to those who are less fortunate. This meant that seeking purpose in life wasn't a difficult endeavor that might or might not result in satisfaction. It turns out that finding meaning is not at all difficult. Happiness is a decision, as many wise people have noted. Happiness is impossible without thanks, my mother once told me. She stated, "When I ask God for happiness, he tells me to learn to be grateful instead." She was correct, as was He.

Chapter 6:
Victimhood and Oppression

I was very resolved to instill in my son the traits of fortitude, gratitude, and happiness that I believed were terribly lacking in many of the Americans my age that I had encountered during my time as a college student. In any event, I would have preferred to raise him in that manner, but I was also aware of the social and professional environment in which he was being born.

When my parents and I lost track of my older sister, Eunmi, who was sixteen at the time, I was thirteen years old. We were all terrified of the very real and impending prospect of famine because we didn't have any food in the house. On March 26, 2007, my sister crossed the Yalu River from Hyesan into China. She had sent me a note telling me to travel to China and look for her.

Our path to reunification was fraught with difficulty and trying challenges. When I was twenty years old, South Korean intelligence placed my sister and I in touch after the horrible horrors of the Chinese sex trade, and we were reunited in Seoul, South Korea. Seven complete years had passed; for girls our age, that was an eternity. We were no longer young adults or teenagers.

The one realization I had early in my life in South Korea was that there is no end to self-pity. This realization enabled me to endure any suffering I continued to encounter and to live life with thankfulness and optimism. No matter how far you sink into self-pity, no matter how much you believe you are benefiting from it or justified in plunging into its depths, there is simply no limit. It's like a bottomless hole or an endless tunnel. If you jump in, it will be difficult for you to get back out again.

Many Americans and other people from across the world have questioned me about how it's possible for me to be thankful for having been born in North Korea, as I stated in my first book. I can see their perplexity. I often respond by saying that I wouldn't be able to appreciate the wealth, justice, safety, and freedom I experience with such intense intensity every day in America if I hadn't endured starvation, injustice, oppression, and the loss of loved ones. Of course, everything depends on perspective, and since I was born in North Korea, I have more than most. And that has made me a better boxer.

I want my son to have the same viewpoint, but I don't want him to go through the same ordeal that I had in order to get it. I thus strive to implant it in him by leading by example and by instructing him as my parents did for me.

However, as any parent is aware, it might be difficult to avoid worrying as you release your children into society, even one as admirable, just, and free as America's, because of the role models and teachers they will encounter there. I also worry about my son.

I've attempted to implant this wisdom in my son since he was just five years old because I know he probably won't learn it in school. Schools in America are increasingly no longer instructing students that pain is either essential or something they can control. The institutions that educate and support us in raising our kids are increasingly emphasizing to them that social oppression, manifest in the shape of American capitalist democracy, is the sole cause of all suffering.

As I hinted at in the introduction, I have faced attacks and accusations of being "right wing" or "far right" for the entirety of my time in the United States, almost exclusively because of what I have said in public regarding the Chinese and North Korean regimes, both of which the U.S. government itself, under various administrations, has characterized as enemies or rivals. However, my criticisms of aspects of American political culture that remind me of the authoritarian inclinations I am so familiar with from my early life have also been a driving force behind such attempts at cancellation. Even while the criticism and charges are rarely univocal, they frequently originate from one political group in particular: Americans who identify as Marxists, Leninists, Maoists, Communists, Socialists, Democratic Socialists, or more broadly, members of "the Left."

Democracy grants everyone the freedom to believe in and advocate for any rubbish they choose. But the reason it worries me is because the same people who have condemned me for speaking against communism beyond the bounds of appropriate political discourse are also frequently the most well-known and powerful figures in the society my small kid will soon inhabit. They are tasked with staffing the educational institutions that are in charge of his education, creating the information environment that is supposed to curate his understanding of the outside world, and delivering many of the social services that his community and he depend on. They also have a strong commitment to leftism, an ideology that is very similar to the one I narrowly managed to escape.

Once more, everyone in America is free to be a fool. But the issue is that the Left has successfully conflated itself with liberalism in the public's mind, collapsing America's once-impressive and crucial left flank—which was once committed to genuine economic solidarity and racial equality—into an oligarchic ideology of economic exploitation and racial division. Many American leftists can promote the superiority of an authoritarian social and political system without ever having to live under it or deal with its repercussions since leftism and liberalism are often conflated. They continue to benefit from democratic capitalism's advantages, such as prosperity, social mobility, freedom of expression and organization, and property ownership, even as they push for its abolition.

This often results in a form of self-hatred and cognitive dissonance that manifests as strident in-group rivalry over who endures great suffering under the current system. For someone like New York representative Alexandria Ocasio-Cortez, for example, the more personal success she accrues—the more profitably she employs American democratic capitalism to realize her personal, professional, reputational, and financial ambitions—the more she feels compelled to act out her own imagined victimization, her own uncontrollable suffering, and her own supposed opposition to the very system she so successfully employs.

The idea that Kim Il Sung, the founding tyrant of North Korea, was not only a superb leader but also a deity helped him gain power. He did so, in part, by pledging to eliminate all types of injustice and inequality, which, in his view, were unimportant, straightforward issues that needed uncomplicated answers. He said that a capitalist plot to make everyone pay for necessities like education, healthcare, shelter, and food—everything people need to exist and thrive—was the primary cause of both inequality and injustice. All kinds of private ownership had to be eliminated in order to make these resources and services available to everyone, which meant that "capitalists" (i.e., regular citizens) were no longer permitted to own their own homes, farms, schools, or hospitals. They were taken away by the state, which is to say, the military and police. As in China, Vietnam, Cuba, the Soviet Union, Yugoslavia, and the Warsaw Pact nations, the outcomes were unquestionably disastrous.

In North Korea, I saw the results of this process firsthand. The upshot of the regime's elimination of private property rights and theft of all the people's possessions was obviously not the free and unrestricted access to the resources and services that ordinary people depend on, but rather the outright theft of those resources by the regime's followers and enforcers. In addition to enriching the dictatorship, this process produced a privileged group of middle-level administrators, managers, military officers, and bureaucrats who greatly value wealth, property, and inequality while still supporting socialist revolution. (I believe you are starting to recognize this.)

I'VE developed a particular interest in attempts to categorize Americans as oppressors or victims in recent years since my kid and I both ended ourselves on the other side of the split from where I had anticipated.

I've never wanted to be treated like a victim in America or anyplace else, and I've never felt like one either. I would have assumed that Asian Americans might fall into the former camp, for obvious historical reasons, if you had told me that the United States is a country where some people are considered victims based on the color of their skin while some are considered oppressors based on the color of their skin.

Asian Americans have a rich and diverse history, but for most of American history, this group was subjected to state-sanctioned racism, exploitation, segregation, and unimaginable civil rights abuses. Does that imply that those who immigrated from Asia during the first few waves now are deemed to have the "blood" of the oppressed?

Quite the opposite. As of the summer of 2022, the US Supreme Court has agreed to hear a case brought by Asian-American college students who claim there is discrimination at Harvard and other prestigious universities, including the use of unofficial quota systems, similar to how the Ivy League upheld Jewish quotas in the early 20th century. In spite of the fact that the Asian-American community is the fastest-growing in the country, the percentage of Asian-American students at Harvard has stayed steady over the previous ten years at 20%. A male non-poor Asian-American applicant with the qualifications to have a 25% chance of admission to Harvard would have a 36% probability if he were white, according to estimates by an economist hired by the plaintiffs in the Supreme Court case. That would be 77% for Hispanics and 95% for Blacks if he were of those races.

In America, leftist ideology (as opposed to liberalism or liberal causes) has grown so blatantly ludicrous and self-contradictory that regular people, especially parents, have shown signs of abandoning it entirely. On the heels of a debate about whether or not parents should have the right to object to the teaching of leftist racial ideology in public schools, Virginia, which is becoming an increasingly blue state, elected a Republican governor in January 2022. The state's former governor, Terry McAuliffe, had rejected legislation requiring schools to alert parents of novel and divisive curricula. "I'm not going to let parents come into schools and actually take books out and make their own decision," McAuliffe vowed during the campaign. Parents shouldn't, in my opinion, dictate what should be taught in schools. The Republican candidate, Glenn Youngkin, ran on the platform that parents should, of course, be involved in their children's education. After Youngkin won the election, MSNBC referred to him, Winsome Sears, his Black female lieutenant governor from Jamaica, and Jason Miyares, his Cuban attorney general, as "white supremacists" for supporting the democratic idea of holding schools accountable to their communities. However, Virginia voters' common sense and basic decency exposed the racist, North Korean-like attempt to characterize any dissent to critical race theory as "oppressive."

Similar to this, San Francisco's voters overwhelmingly decided to recall all three of the city's school board members in February 2022. Over 70% of the vote, an astounding majority, was cast in favor of the recall. The city's poorest and most vulnerable students suffered significant learning losses as a result of the school board's decision to keep public schools closed to in-person instruction throughout the pandemic, all the while debating whether to rename any buildings named after prominent white supremacists like Abraham Lincoln. The school board also abolished test score requirements for Lowell, the most prominent and successful public high school in the city, where Asian American students have been overrepresented and hence unfairly punished. Voters in San Francisco were OK to communist philosophy as long as it only affected other people; however, when it started to affect their children, they had had enough.

As my son joins the New York school system, which is not renowned for either its sanity or its capacity to remain above the political battle, I do worry for him. But I'm encouraged by the example set by parents in Virginia and San Francisco, who not only saw past the American left's fraudulence but also showed their continued faith in democracy by turning out to the polls and taking charge of their neighborhoods. Convenient justifications that they were being oppressed or victimized by outside forces did not satisfy them. They acknowledged their errors, accepted responsibility for them, and resolved to do better moving forward.

I therefore have some optimism for my kid and his generation as they approach the start of the school year. I'll make sure he receives the education he needs and deserves in any case.

The safety of both he and I, though, is something I feel I have less control over.

Chapter 7:
Systemic Violence in the Windy City

I never came across a globe map throughout the thirteen years I spent living in North Korea. I also never learned anything about any other nationalities than the American Bastards and Japanese imperialists. So it stands to reason that I was ignorant of the actual number of nations and ethnic groups on Earth. Until American Bastards were extinguished by God, Kim Il Sung, North Korea was like the sun, the center of the solar system, and all other peoples circled around it.

Many moons later, I believed my brain was going to go supernova when I learnt about the nations of the globe, the Earth, the solar system, the Milky Way galaxy, and the constantly expanding universe. Think of describing a fidget spinner to a Martian extraterrestrial. Trying to explain planetary systems to a North Korean is analogous to doing that.

Of course, there's a valid explanation for that in addition to North Korean education's deficiencies. What are the origins of matter, energy, and theories of space and time to a person whose stomach grumbles at night to prevent her from falling asleep rather than trying to discover a solution to her imminent starvation? For the first half of my life, my body frequently spoke with me in this manner, and whenever it did, I frequently turned to the sky and prayed for compassion, thinking that something, anything, up there could hear me. I would ask for a miracle, hoping that a door in the firmament would miraculously open and food would fall from the sky and land on my lap. My sole interaction with the stars was through this.

One of the first privileges I learned to value when I immigrated to America was my newly discovered freedom of mobility. When I needed food, I could just go to the store on foot; when I wanted to see friends or a new location, I could take the train; and when I wanted to go to other areas of the nation, meet other Americans, and take in new vistas and landscapes, I could simply get in a car or fly. It's challenging to describe how unique this freedom truly is if you have never envied a bird, even a pigeon—which I assume the majority of people haven't).

I made use of this freedom in the beginning of 2019 while still enrolled as a senior at Columbia and moved to Chicago, Illinois, with my husband. Prior to the relocation, I frequently traveled to the Windy City because my husband's company had a location there. There, I had also given birth to my son.

Initially, I had pondered working for international organizations like the United Nations, but as time went on, I lost faith in their efficacy and eventually lost all comprehension of why the UN even existed. North Korea's government continues to be a full member of the UN, which entitles it to one vote per country in the General Assembly. It has been permitted to preside over nuclear disarmament panels and vote on human rights resolutions! Every year since 2005, the General Assembly has passed a resolution denouncing the state of human rights in North Korea, but of course, this has accomplished absolutely nothing. These pointless resolutions, whose only apparent goal is to allow self-admiring diplomats and bureaucrats to praise one another for being so virtuous, have never benefitted a single victim of the Kim dictatorship.

Chicago was then placed under lockdown in March. A shelter-in-place order was issued by the mayor on March 20. Businesses and schools were closed. At this point, masks were still regarded as useless, and if you weren't a member of the medical profession, buying one was seen as selfish. Finally, it became unlawful to leave your house without a mask. Grocery stores and other indoor establishments remained open while kid-friendly playgrounds and other outside areas were shut down. The administration emphasized the value of "contact tracing," but never really seemed to put it into practice. Although it mentioned the need for universal testing, it continued to effectively render quick, simple, and inexpensive at-home testing unlawful for the first year by encircling the manufacturers in red tape. Because they either followed or disobeyed orders from the government, which were always changing, Americans called each other traitors. It was a mess.

However, the pandemic very soon split many Americans along cultural and political lines. It didn't help that it was an election year and that Donald Trump was a very divisive president, sparking either passionate allegiance or extreme hatred in supporters eager to credit him with everything that went well or to paint him with everything that went wrong. America is like a huge, exposed, raw nerve.

Then, less than a week after I received my diploma on May 25, 2020, a police officer in Minneapolis killed George Floyd, an unarmed Black man.

Between May 29 and June 1, Chicago experienced rioting and looting on successive nights as a result of the protests that followed Floyd's murder. The "Magnificent Mile" on Michigan Avenue and a number of small shops and businesses in downtown Chicago were utterly destroyed. Among the destroyed and burned buildings and stores were pharmacies, children's hospitals, and nonprofit organizations. Every night there were fatal shootings, and the sirens of responding police, fire, and ambulance vehicles never seemed to stop. All of the bridges spanning the Chicago River were raised as a result of several dangers to the city's infrastructure. My neighborhood in downtown Chicago was the only one connected to other areas of the city by a heavily secured bridge. We had to cross the city through a number of checkpoints throughout the day, and there were curfews at night.

My spouse walked outside one day during the unrest to observe the situation firsthand. Nearly every store on Michigan Avenue, which is only a few blocks from our house, was being looted or was the target of attempted looting. (Notable outliers included the fly fishing retailer Orvis and Banana Republic.) A rampant theft was taking place while several police officers were outside. The mayor reportedly gave the police instructions not to confront the looters until violent crimes were committed.

However, the pandemic very soon split many Americans along cultural and political lines. It didn't help that it was an election year and that Donald Trump was a very divisive president, sparking either passionate allegiance or extreme hatred in supporters eager to credit him with everything that went well or to paint him with everything that went wrong. America is like a huge, exposed, raw nerve.

Then, less than a week after I received my diploma on May 25, 2020, a police officer in Minneapolis killed George Floyd, an unarmed Black man.

Between May 29 and June 1, Chicago experienced rioting and looting on successive nights as a result of the protests that followed Floyd's murder. The "Magnificent Mile" on Michigan Avenue and a number of small shops and businesses in downtown Chicago were utterly destroyed. Among the destroyed and burned buildings and stores were pharmacies, children's hospitals, and nonprofit organizations. Every night there were fatal shootings, and the sirens of responding police, fire, and ambulance vehicles never seemed to stop. All of the bridges spanning the Chicago River were raised as a result of several dangers to the city's infrastructure. My neighborhood in downtown Chicago was the only one connected to other areas of the city by a heavily secured bridge. We had to cross the city through a number of checkpoints throughout the day, and there were curfews at night.

My spouse walked outside one day during the unrest to observe the situation firsthand. Nearly every store on Michigan Avenue, which is only a few blocks from our house, was being looted or was the target of attempted looting. (Notable outliers included the fly fishing retailer Orvis and Banana Republic.) A rampant theft was taking place while several police officers were outside. The mayor reportedly gave the police instructions not to confront the looters until violent crimes were committed.

The official American progressive ideology, which went into overdrive in the summer of 2020, also had some striking disingenuity in common with North Korea. It is not unusual for a farmer in North Korea who is on the verge of starvation to hear the well-fed son of a Party official criticize him for his lack of devotion to the Dear Leader. In America's "racial reckoning" of 2020, it suddenly became OK, for instance, for a white magazine editor to criticize a Black construction worker who intended to vote for the incorrect presidential candidate for his "internalized racism."

On August 14, a gorgeous day in Chicago, I chose to take my two-year-old son and our nanny, a young Muslim woman who wears a headscarf, for a stroll down Michigan Avenue. By that time, we had spent a lot of time indoors, so I wanted my youngster to enjoy some fresh air by venturing back outside.

Just a block from Jane Byrne Park on the Magnificent Mile, at a little after four, I saw that people were closely following me. I looked around and noticed two women. They quickly surrounded me, and one of the women pushed me against a marble pillar that was affixed to the exterior of a building. The second woman struck me hard in the chest as she pinned me up against the pillar and searched my pocketbook for my wallet. One of the women knocked my phone out of my hand and flung it into the street when I attempted to call the police. I grabbed one of the women's arms and began to call for assistance, pleading with my nanny to take my son inside the adjacent Macy's. He had witnessed the woman punching me and was visibly terrified.

After they left me and began to flee with my wallet, I ran outside to get my phone and began to record them as they fled while yelling that they had just robbed me. As I was trying to contact the police and recording her, one of them turned around and yelled that I was being racist for trying to do so. She yelled at me, "A person's skin color doesn't make them a thief!" She must have heard a woman on the sidewalk, who just appeared to be a spectator, and she began constantly yelling "Racist!" at me. My two robbers were both Black ladies.

The altercation created quite a scene because Michigan Avenue is a very congested and bustling roadway, but by this time it had taken on a very distinct and breathtakingly ludicrous valence. Many onlookers began yelling at me, and they appeared to be of all races. Particularly, I recall a white mom telling her teenage children at a bus stop—presumably her own—that they were seeing racism in action while glancing over at me.

Within 30 minutes of my calling the police, they showed up and graciously offered to give me medical attention, which I politely declined. They advised me not to fight back in circumstances like this since life itself is more important and that I was lucky not to have been shot or stabbed. They took my statement, and after finding the attacker who had attacked me, they made me choose her from a lineup. (After the argument, she used my credit card in cabs and shops, leaving the cops with an easy trail to follow.) I made the decision to accuse her. She later admitted to having numerous past convictions, including one for serious battery, and to having engaged in wrongful restraint. Prosecutors agreed to remove the robbery charge as part of the plea deal, and she received a two-year prison term in return. The incident was eventually covered by the tabloid the Daily Mail, who also published the attacker's name and identification. This, I was warned, was not the best course of action because "revenge crime" and "revenge murders" are frequent occurrences in Chicago.

I still don't understand why, out of all the people on Michigan Avenue that day, they chose to attack me. Given all the other physical assaults on Asian Americans that increased that summer— again, according to the most recent crime data, approximately a quarter of the violent assailants were Black, approximately a quarter were White, approximately a quarter were Latino and "other" combined, and approximately a quarter were Asian—I suppose it's not really a big surprise. I'm still baffled by the actions of the onlookers, none of whom had the decency to even verbally support a young mother who was being attacked in the street in front of her son, instead opting to insult her and encourage the assailants. It demonstrated to me how far the awakened illness had spread in America at that time and how cruel it was turning normally normal individuals. The sole contribution that the woke movement has made to American society is to base decisions on whether or not to provide assistance, dignity, or physical safety on the basis of a person's skin color. It would cause the Civil Rights Movement heroes of the United States to turn in their graves.

Chapter 8:
What's Yours Is Mine

One of the things that struck me the most during my first trip to the United States in 2013 was the incredible degree of plenty there. Even in Tyler, Texas, which has a population of 106,000 and is the 299th largest city in the country, there were shops and enterprises peddling a wide variety of products and services. Tyler is a very tiny city in Texas. Everywhere I turned, I saw brand-new, attractive goods that were expertly branded and packaged and were ready for sale or consumption. If a store was low on a certain item around the end of a work day, it would be back up to full capacity by early the following morning, as if by magic.

We had jangmadang (dark markets) in North Korea, where we occasionally found luxury items like Chinese imitation handbags and sneakers, as well as some basic requirements like dried food. Even when I fled and eventually settled in South Korea, I might have discovered one or two possibilities for a specific kind of goods in a typical Seoul store. But in America, there seemed to be nearly endless possibilities for every single commodity. There were more than a dozen different varieties of apples in a normal big-box grocery shop—not a fancy, specialized organic food store, just your average HEB supermarket—all with enticing names like Honeycrisp, Gala, Pink Lady, Fuji, and Granny Smith. For packaged goods like toothpaste, it seemed that every firm offered a variety of flavors for consumers with various tastes and life phases. I discovered that there is no such thing as a "toothbrush" in America. Soft, medium, and firm bristles, motorized and manual, boy and female, youngsters and adults, Star Wars and Toy Story are all available. The sheer amount of options occasionally paralyzed me. What if I chose incorrectly? Or was it simply a poor choice? I wasn't accustomed to having to choose between so many options so frequently throughout a typical day.

A lot of the things I saw for sale also eluded me as to why they were even there. It had never occurred to me to peel fruit, which can be done with a fruit peeler, or to cook food in a cast-iron Crock Pot rather than in a bowl or on a plate. By the way, I've now changed my mind and now love both of these products! And capitalism is brilliant in this regard. The key behind all of these items is that they wouldn't have been created in the first place if they weren't filling a genuine demand among regular people. Market demand is present, providers satiate that desire, and consumers gain. Businesses profit from the difference between the retail price and the cost of items sold after setting up a supply chain and compensating each node for its contribution. Millions of tiny micro-economies, wonderfully on show in every aisle and on every shelf of an American storefront, make up the entire economic value chain.

As I spent more time in America, particularly in New York, a city that serves as a melting pot for immigrant groups from across the globe, I realized that capitalism not only drives the American economy but also the global economy. Consumers aren't the only ones who benefit from capitalism; it has also helped billions of others escape hunger and poverty. Additionally, it is the most democratic and equitable system that people have so far created. Every consumer "votes" in a capitalist society by spending their hard-earned money on the goods they like, which is frequently a much better indicator of their true, strongly held views than casting a ballot. For example, if you oppose child labor, you can refuse to buy products made by children; if you favor a particular method of farming or manufacturing, you can purchase goods from businesses that use it; if you favor a weaker foreign nation, you can purchase its imports.

Very few capitalist ideas even exist in North Korea (the Kim regime, for instance, forbids the word profit). However, those that do exist show how much more in tune with human nature they are than any of the other ideologies. This is best appreciated in light of the underground economy that exists in North Korea (as well as in every other civilization that has ever been), where people naturally learn how to trade and barter like ideal capitalist merchants and captains of industry. In Hyesan, my father was given a factory position that was a complete dead end because the facility was shut down and just produced carbon emissions. My father began trading for himself, despite always prioritizing feeding his wife and girls. This was a very risky decision. First, he bought and sold cigarettes and dried fish. He began transferring metals and smuggling them into China when the margins weren't profitable enough. For a while, our family prospered by North Korean standards because of this lucrative but extremely risky operation.

As I detailed in In Order to Live, my mother gave me a small business loan to help me get off the ground. I used it to get some rice vodka to bribe the guard at a government-run persimmon plantation. He let my sister and I sneak into the orchard to collect some fruit after receiving the vodka. We transported the persimmons back to Kowon in a large metal bucket over many miles, where I sold them in the jangmadang, the famine-era markets that sprang up all over North Korea.

Milton Friedman, a researcher at the University of Chicago who received the Nobel Prize in Economic Sciences in 1976, was one of the most important economists of the 20th century. In a previous essay, Friedman claimed that "the only cases in which the masses have escaped grinding poverty, are where they have had capitalism and largely free trade." This is true even for communist nations like China, where hundreds of millions of people were able to escape poverty and illiteracy as a result of the Cultural Revolution's narrow, limited introduction of capitalism and free markets. It was true of the Central and Eastern European countries that, after 1990, were finally able to liberate themselves from the Soviet Union's burden and went on to become wealthy and successful countries. The richest nation in human history, the United States, is a prime example.

Anyone who has had to file business taxes with the IRS or apply for numerous business licenses from America's countless regulatory agencies may not realize it right away, but the United States is remarkably pro-business, especially when compared to the rest of the globe. No economic system in the world is more supportive to entrepreneurs, which is why more innovators, artists, and visionaries relocate to America than to any other nation. Regulations are burdensome, and not all incentives are perfectly aligned. Ask them to explain why there are more visa, green card, and citizenship applications made to the United States than to any other nation in the world if you know someone who believes that America is particularly xenophobic and racist.

In modern America, some people believe that "business" and "investing" are somehow related to "fraud." These folks don't realize that being an entrepreneur entails more than just coming up with a creative strategy to make money, such as buying your way into an orchard and then reselling the fruit to customers. It is a method of discovering a fundamental human need and figuring out how to meet it, thereby producing goods, services, and jobs for other people— people who may someday have their own ideas but who almost always have their own families to feed, houses to build and buy, and taxes to pay—and who may one day have their own ideas. Whether such benefits are in the millions or billions, it goes without saying that prosperous businesspeople should be compensated with the financial gains from the social goods and services they produce.

The values of entrepreneurship, free enterprise, starting a business, and doing well are sacrosanct to someone like me who was born in North Korea, as well as to billions of other people throughout the world, and there is no limit to how much good they can do. They are also very smart and complicated! Learning how the New York Stock Exchange operates is comparable to learning fifth-dimensional string theory for a North Korean immigrant. To gain as much knowledge about contemporary economics, business, and finance as possible in the shortest amount of time was one of the key reasons I chose to study economics at Columbia.

Another Milton Friedman quotation I adore is this one: "A society that prioritizes equality over freedom will achieve neither." A society with a high degree of both will choose freedom over equality. The core of socialism, according to Friedman, is the idea that societies that place a high priority on equality never raise those at the bottom to the top but instead drive everyone as far down as they can go. On the other hand, societies that value freedom naturally produce a considerably higher level of genuine equality than the socialist system. Which is better: a society where there is extreme inequality between the typical person's yearly income of $65,000 and the top 1%'s annual income of $500,000, or a society where everyone is treated equally with an annual income of $4,000?

Unfortunately, this issue is particularly pronounced in the Democratic-dominated cities that have pervasive corruption and little to no political opposition. It is less surprising that it is more noticeable in cities with elected authorities who identify as socialist or anti-capitalist. It never seems to work out that the better the schools or the lower the crime, the bluer the city hall or the mayor's home is in New York, Chicago, Los Angeles, San Francisco, Detroit, or Baltimore.

My worry about money is a little aspect of a bigger question that has been on my mind ever since I escaped North Korea and attained freedom. It has to do with the prosperity of the country. How do countries succeed and accumulate genuine economic, scientific, and cultural wealth? There is a historical instance that, in my opinion, hints at a potential solution.

History lovers are aware that the Mongol Empire, which rose in the thirteenth century, was one of the most spectacular empires ever created. The Mongol Empire reached as far west as Central Europe and the Black Sea in addition to the Pacific Ocean in the east. At their peak extent, they are thought to have seized 24 million square kilometers of land, which is larger than the combined areas of the United States, Brazil, and Australia. They are believed to have taken all of modern-day China and a large portion of northern Russia before moving south to the Indian subcontinent. Uneducated tribesmen traveling on horseback and living in yurts, not technological superiority, which was the driving force behind the European imperial enterprise that started in the seventeenth century, were responsible for this amazing accomplishment of imperial expansion.

How did a so-called "primitive civilization" conquer and rule over more advanced societies like Persia and Byzantium? Meritocracy, in a single word.

Naturally, I oppose all forms of harsh execution, including rape, pillaging, and imperial invasion. The notion that meritocracy is essential to national survival and success is an old one, and I believe that to be important. Even the Chinese Communist Party has embraced merit; it bases admittance into the civil service, appointments, and promotions on rigorous testing. Leftists in America regularly condemn merit itself as being somehow identical with racial privilege. The provision of public goods is viewed as requiring demonstrable talent, hard effort, and dedication, whether it is managing health services in a hamlet, managing foreign investment in a municipal district, or supervising in a state-sponsored company. In China, performance is evaluated once a year through in-depth interviews by superiors, colleagues, and subordinates who also conduct public opinion polls to gauge workers' competency.

These are for regular civil service positions, including those at the DMV, in the Chinese bureaucracy. However, the Communist Party views public administration expertise as a necessity for national success and, therefore, as a survival tactic.

The unsavory truth about left-wing criticisms of capitalism, the family, and the meritocracy in America is that they are seen as quite the funny joke in China, which enjoys seeing Americans minimize and denigrate all of their assets.

Chapter 9:
The Terror of Cancel Culture

To share my thoughts and findings from my investigation into North Korea's situation and China's support of the Kim dictatorship, I launched the Voice of North Korea by Yeonmi Park YouTube channel in August 2020. Online participation was extraordinarily high because the pandemic was in full flow and millions of people were still under some kind of lockdown when I launched the channel. 100,000 users subscribed to the channel in just two months. This is what I had long desired: a global platform that would enable me to speak directly to a sizable audience of individuals all over the world, as opposed to traveling to various conferences and private events where I could only briefly catch the attention of a select number of influential people. In my first half-decade in America, I'd learned that attempting to sway decision-makers' actions or behaviors using my own life experience was a fruitless endeavor. Through mutual education and interaction between many regular people, real change must occur. The internet was created with the intention of fulfilling this promise, and my plan was to do so by creating an "army of kindred spirits" to combat the evil of these two communist regimes.

I started off by primarily making descriptive and human-interest movies, such as ten- to fifteen-minute pieces about North Korean cuisine, the cultural shock I'd gone through when I first moved to the United States, introducing viewers to other North Korean defectors, and the like. Then I began to create videos that introduced the viewer to the North Korean regime itself, including an explanation of the nation's gulag system, a section on Kim Jong Un's vicious and enigmatic sister, and a clip on how the regime generates income. Three million people saw a film I made in September 2020 about Ri Sol Ju, Kim Jong Un's wife and the first lady of North Korea. "Daily Life of a North Korean," a video I made in October, attracted nearly six million views. I saw in it a possibility to both expand my activism and make a small living by monetizing the videos with adverts as the channel truly seemed to be taking off.

However, something startling occurred that troubled year when fall gave way to winter. In addition to North Korea itself, I began to film documentaries about Chinese support for the dictatorship there as well as the plight of North Koreans, particularly women, who reside in China. These videos were all quickly demonetized by YouTube. YouTube demonetized my films on the COVID-19 origin controversy as well as the Chinese danger to international security. Demonetization even affected a film I made about the Second Amendment that has nothing to do with China. I also noticed that more and more of my friends and followers were alerting me to the possibility that my Instagram account, which I used to update followers on my activism, book tours, and collaborative projects, was being shadow-banned. This meant that it was frequently challenging to locate my account even if you searched for it by name.

The United States may have been founded in the late eighteenth century as a response to monarchical tyranny, but its origins go back an additional century and a half. It was an exodus in quest of truth and freedom that the English religious exiles made when they decided to make the challenging and perilous trek across the Atlantic to the New World. They made sacrifices for their search that were nearly inconceivable. They began on an uncertain journey after leaving behind everything they had ever known. The winter was unbearably brutal when they arrived in Massachusetts, and the terrain of dense forests and woods was severe. No visible source of food or shelter existed, and neither did any authority or security. Everything had to be constructed from the ground up.

Making people second-guess their every action out of concern for their jobs has a name. It is referred to as "dictatorship of the mind." The Kim government recognized early on that if ordinary Koreans lacked the language necessary to express their servitude, they would not be able to interpret or comprehend it. There are therefore no words in official North Korean for oppression, trauma, depression, or love—only synonyms for the "socialist paradise." Since they lack the words to describe or envision a new way of life, millions of North Koreans may be hungry and afraid.

The goal of canceling culture in America is to deny people their ability or right to communicate ideas that conflict with official narratives, eventually to the point where they are unable to do so. If you scare people enough that criticizing the incorrect thing would ruin their reputations and livelihoods, ultimately they won't even know what to criticize.

I should have known better, but I didn't, and it cost me. Whether these judgments were made by humans or algorithms, attempts to cancel me did not end with YouTube demonetizing my videos or Instagram and Twitter presumably shadow-banning my accounts. There was growing pressure for formerly sympathetic organizations to exclude me on the grounds that I was too controversial as I publicly criticized the Chinese government—mostly for its role in the sexual enslavement of North Korean women, hardly a "controversial" position.

For instance, toward the end of 2021, I received an invitation to speak about my upbringing in North Korea at Samsung Semiconductor, Inc., a Samsung Electronics subsidiary based in San Jose, California. I agreed to the offer, and my speech there was slated for January 25, 2022. The speech topic was listed on the invitation, which was sent to about 200 Samsung employees, as "Yeonmi's story of escaping North Korea," and it was a part of a series dubbed "Speaker series hosted by Women in Samsung Electronics." It was a rather routine situation.

But on January 13, I got an email informing me that the speech had been postponed. The email states that Yeonmi had been approved for booking by Samsung's event coordinator, but when the contract was being completed, an executive protested, claiming that she would be too "political." This went up the ladder, and now they are urging that they must cancel.

I can personally attest that it is not just a fad or a foolish new front in a childish culture war because I have withstood multiple attempts at cancellation. With the aid of contemporary technologies, American culture has come a long way toward achieving what no democratic regime is capable of achieving on its own and what every dictatorial regime throughout history has mastered: making people with opposing opinions vanish at the touch of a button.

Now have a look at my lone video where I criticize the Chinese government, which is regarded as an enemy regime of the US. YouTube demonetized the video without a trial, judge or jury, verdict, or sentence—in other words, without a fair trial. My account has occasionally been purportedly shadow blocked by Instagram. Because of my unfavorable comments, organizations that had invited me to talk about my own life abruptly withdrew their invites. With the click of a button, I was deprived of my ability to earn an honest income despite having no charges or convictions.

Cancel culture is barring regular people from participating in society if their beliefs are deemed "undesirable" by the media, businesses, and the government, rather than just seeking to penalize comedians for occasionally making tasteless jokes (which is their right to do). It's as grave as grave gets.

What we can do about this new union of corporate, financial, technological, and political power that imperils our judicial system is difficult to tell. One is to pray that more decentralized technologies will be created and adopted widely, weaning us off of our reliance on Big Tech. Another is to entirely withdraw from the Big Tech sector—leaving Twitter, Facebook, and all the other sites that support mob rule.

Reaffirming our commitment to the fundamental values of our Founding Fathers and their ancestors, such as freedom of assembly, expression, and speech, is a more modest request. This entails placing the law above our own feelings, as the ACLU did in Skokie, Illinois. Additionally, it entails protecting people's rights from the mob, including those whose opinions we disagree with.

In other words, we have to choose the difficult route. If the truth demands it, we too must travel the difficult, uncharted, and frightening path that the pilgrims did. Because there is no other way to achieve freedom.

Chapter 10:
The People's Republic of Chains

Unquestionably, the Chinese economic growth miracle of the past two decades is among the most remarkable and significant events in contemporary international history. Modern China, also known as "the red dragon," has emerged as the largest or second-largest force in world trade and business. The tenacity of hundreds of millions of common Chinese people deserves a great deal of credit for this amazing effort. But the filthy methods used by the government also play a significant role in the explanation. In addition to innovation, the Chinese Communist Party has secured the nation's manufacturing hegemony through low-cost production made possible by pitifully low wages and appalling working conditions. It has mastered large-scale, inexpensive shipping through effective logistics as well as through influencing global supply chains—often illegally—to offer China a competitive advantage over the United States, Europe, and other key markets. In spite of the substantial domestic legitimacy needed to maintain the regime, this combination has led to considerable global instability. China has rescued more people from poverty during the 1980s than the entire rest of the globe combined.

China's reputation abroad derives from a variety of sources. Due to its participation on the victorious side of World War II, it is still a permanent member of the United Nations Security Council and one of only five nations in the world with veto power over joint resolutions. In terms of technology and science, China is likewise in the forefront. It already leads the world in infrastructure like high-speed rail, payments, online retail, and these industries will likely soon take over consumer electronics. Additionally, China stands a chance of dominating in the fields of artificial intelligence and quantum computing, which would undoubtedly support its increasing military might. Only the United States spent more on defense in 2021 ($240 billion), and China had the largest active military force ever with over two million soldiers.

These are impressive accomplishments for a nation that describes itself as a "unitary, single-party, socialist state"—a political and economic model with an unblemished historical record of failure, collapse, and defeat outside of China. And it's not like China doesn't have the same flaws as every other communist government that has existed and fallen.

Only Turkmenistan, Eritrea, and—you guessed it—North Korea were worse for "freedom of the press" in 2020 than China, according to the NGO Reporters Without Borders. China ranked #129 in the 2020 Human Freedom Index of the CATO Institute, which examines 76 different indices of individual and economic freedom. The only nations that collectively scored the same as or lower than China on qualitative freedom indexes were Cuba, Turkmenistan, Iran, Iraq, and North Korea (the "Axis of Evil"). Even in the Heritage Foundation's rating of economic and business freedom, China came in at number 107.

For China, the early modern era was not favorable. China fell prey to Western imperial ambitions by the nineteenth century, when the European colonial empires had far outperformed it in almost all dimensions of power—economic, military, and technological. Early in the 20th century, China was a nation without a political or economic future; nearly all of its enormous people lived in utter poverty, and many were purposefully turned opium addicts by Western powers, especially the United States. The British, Americans, Germans, Russians, French, Japanese, and others all vied for power during this time, reducing China to little more than a Western sphere of influence.

China joined the Entente (France, Britain, and Russia) in World War I in 1917. China's contribution to the alliance was primarily laborers who labored in the mines and factories of the alliance. However, the Treaty of Versailles, the post-war peace signed by the war's winners, disregarded China's requests to put an end to its nightmare of foreign rule. For instance, the treaty essentially gave Japan control of Chinese territory that had been controlled by the vanquished German Empire rather than returning it to the Chinese people.

Three thousand Chinese students protested the Treaty of Versailles on May 4, 1919, in Tiananmen Square. The May Fourth Movement was a part of a larger cultural movement that promoted scientific endeavors, enhanced literacy, and more egalitarian, populist political participation in order to replace traditional Chinese society and values with more modern and forward-looking ones. The May Fourth Movement gave rise to the Chinese Communist Party, which was soon established.

Meanwhile, in northeastern China's Manchuria, Imperial Japan invaded, annexed the region in 1931, and created the puppet state of Manchukuo. Most historians believe that World War II began on July 7, 1937, when fighting broke out between the Republic of China and Imperial Japan, not when Hitler invaded Poland more than two years later. By 1939, Chiang had blockaded the communists in the northwest while Japan controlled the majority of China's east coast. After so many years of war, occupation, economic hardship, and mounting inflation, the United States finally intervened on behalf of nationalist China in 1944, but the nationalists were still in a weak position at the time.

China experienced what is generally regarded as the worst famine in human history between 1958 and 1962. Between 15 and 55 million people perished from starvation as a direct result of Mao's land and property policies, which were a component of the Great Leap Forward. In an apparent effort to rid China of any intellectual opposition to communism and Mao's totalitarian rule, up to 20 million Chinese were killed during the Cultural Revolution, which began in 1966 under the leadership of Mao and the CCP. 90% of Chinese people were living in extreme poverty by the time Mao passed away in September 1976, earning less than $2 a day, and almost everyone had lost a parent, grandparent, child, or sibling to famine or genocide. Mao stands out even in the history of global communism and fascism, which has produced monsters and mass murders on par with Hitler, Stalin, Pol Pot, and the Kims. Up to 78 million people are believed to have died as a result of Mao's rule, policies, government, and leadership. The "socialist paradise."

The miraculous then happened. Following Mao, Deng Xiaoping established a number of capitalist reforms. He established constrained free markets, welcomed foreign investment, and gave many individuals the freedom to pick the employment they desired and didn't want. Over the subsequent decades, as China's economy grew freer and more open, it thrived more and the CCP reclaimed its lost legitimacy. In the three decades following the start of Deng's administration, nearly one billion people were pulled out of poverty. Chinese cities rose to international standards, Chinese science and technology advanced, and the Chinese middle class grew to be the biggest in the world.

When my mother and I were smuggled from North Korea to this prison, it was unfortunate that we were both detained there. I went to China in search of my sister, but I also went there for the one thing that could make my life better on its own: a bowl of rice. At the age of thirteen, I became a man's housekeeper and sex slave in exchange for that pitifully meager luxury, and I had to witness my own mother being regularly pillaged by other men.

I still feel physically sick just thinking about it. But as I become older, the sickness I feel is more tied to the awareness that it's still occurring to numerous other women and girls in China right now, as you read these words. One threat provides their prisoners with the authority and control they require to keep them in servitude: "I will report you to the police if you don't do as I tell you."

The CCP and the Kim family had a particular bond during the Korean War when China and Russia actively assisted Kim Il Sung in his efforts to "unify Korea" under the communist banner. The truth is that an American bombing raid in 1950 resulted in the death in action of Mao Zedong's son. (According to legend, Mao grabbed eggs to prepare himself egg fried rice on the night he passed away despite being forbidden from cooking at night to prevent being seen from the air, alerting American bombers to his unit's location and ultimately leading to their deaths. Nowadays, disobedient Chinese internet users submit recipes for egg fried rice to taunt the government on the anniversary of Mao's son's passing, which the authorities immediately erase.)

Though the fact that a state committed to deposing American dominance will control a significant portion of the Earth's area and population is already frightening, the nature of this new power is far more so. China may be one of the most powerful economic development forces in history, but it comes at a price that even economic growth cannot support. As many nations in Africa, the Balkans, and Latin America have begun to understand, the expansion of Chinese influence also entails an increase in exploitation of workers, destruction of the environment, devastating debt accumulation, inadequate infrastructure, and sex trafficking. Without a question, the growth of Chinese hegemony poses a terrible and dangerous future for almost every nation in the world.

Therefore, it is the responsibility of the only other superpower in the world, the United States of America, to put a stop to it. Sadly, America has been undermined in recent years.

The truth is that the Chinese have acquired a sizable portion of America's elite classes and most productive industries. To keep their revenues rising, Wall Street, Hollywood, Big Tech, and colleges all rely on Chinese markets and money. Their actions over the past two decades are strikingly similar to those of Russia in the 1990s, when Boris Yeltsin's regime saw a small number of oligarchs plunder and sell off the nation's riches in order to enrich themselves, leaving the majority of Russians in a state of anarchy and poverty.

The United States is the only country with a chance of stopping the rise of Chinese dominance, but American elites are actively undermining American economic and military strength in order to enrich themselves. There will simply be no chance to stop a future where China rules the world if this process keeps going. It is impossible for me to adequately express how depressing this is given that I am from North Korea. Exhibit A of what a more Chinese world would look like is the nightmare of North Korea, which is characterized by horrific criminality, excruciating human misery, and the terrifying exploitation of helpless citizens for the benefit of communist party cadres. Chinese hegemony merely promises to increase the number of individuals who have experienced North Korea, not put an end to the misery there.

Chapter 11:
Real Tyranny and Real Freedom

Now that I'm twenty-nine years old and have lived in my new home for the past eight years, with my English getting better every day, I feel like I've finally reached a place where I can express in words what freedom and slavery are, as well as roughly what it's like to live in North Korea. I'm attempting to accurately portray what it's like to be a slave in that nation through books, movies, and talks. I think it's crucial to do this because, as an escaped slave, a free woman, and an American, I have a responsibility and a right to reclaim the words I was never given to define the slavery I experienced as a child and that of the unfortunate people who are still held there.

North Korea is a socialist state and the last holdout of the Marxist-Leninist dream of a communist end to human history. It is a totalitarian dictatorship with nuclear weapons that has imprisoned 26 million people and created a cult of personality around three evil men—two of whom are now deceased—who oversaw a concentration camp the size of a small country. A natural calamity, like in Haiti or Bangladesh, colonial imperialism, like in the Belgian Congo, or ethnic and religious factionalism, like in Syria or Iraq, are not to blame for the squalid nightmare that has played out within its borders every minute, every second, for seventy-four years. It is the world's longest-running experiment in purposefully managed human suffering, a never-ending offense against God, a continuing violation of human dignity, and a stain on humanity so profound and dark that it can almost make you ashamed to be a part of it. Individuals imprisoned there may spend the entirety of their brief lives daydreaming and dreaming of living instead as a bird or even a mouse.

In our very bodies, North Korea's evil is manifest. The genetically identical Korean ethnic group has been divided into different physical categories due to the frequent lack of access to food and basic nutrients for North Koreans, including children and babies. As a result, the communist Koreans live shorter lives than their capitalist brethren, grow to shorter heights and reach lower weights, with all the associated consequences for rates of organ failure, susceptibility to disease, and cognitive function. All the selflessness, generosity, and goodness in the world won't be able to undo the harm, as very little of the food aid that is provided to North Korea actually reaches the hands and mouths of those who are malnourished, food insecure, or on the verge of starvation. The elite in Pyongyang, who have publicly boasted of having accomplished the astounding task of feeding 10% of the population during times of famine, intercept, hold, and ration the great majority of the help.

There is a good reason why North Korea is referred to as the "hermit kingdom." There is no internet, radio, or television that the government does not directly and thoroughly control. In North Korea, every news broadcast and other piece of programming is intended to ensnare the audience in a never-ending loop of propaganda and brainwashing. When they finally understand that Americans do not, in reality, have horns or frigid, slimy, reptilian skin, as they do in every North Korean representation, many defectors experience genuine astonishment. The sheer volume of vehicles that have been clogging the roadways of South Korea and America for many years astounds defectors just as much. The biggest shock of all may come when defectors discover—and eventually accept—that North Korea did not "win" the Korean War and that there was no nuclear explosion at the conflict's conclusion. The best comparison I can even come up with to characterize a North Korean defector's experience is swallowing the red pill in The Matrix.

There isn't a single civil right to which you are entitled in North Korea, even if you remain silent, keep to yourself, and accept your fate, including the fact that you don't have enough food to eat. The bar for being sent to a camp is so low it's almost absurd. Three generations of a family can be rounded up, detained, and executed "to wipe out the seed of dissent" if the authorities notice that dust has accumulated in the corners of a frame holding a portrait of the Dear Leader or if a kid is seen singing a song that has not been approved by the government. Never, ever question why you are in a North Korean concentration camp. That is the first rule. It may lengthen your sentence, bring you closer to death, or result in the arrest and detention of your loved ones. Hwang Jang-yop, a senior official, escaped from North Korea in 1997. In any case, Hwang was the one who developed the Juche philosophy, and the Washington Post later compared his escape to Joseph Goebbels defecting from Nazi Germany. The rest of his family—many of whom were unaware they were related to him—were deported to concentration camps shortly after his wife allegedly committed "suicide," his daughter allegedly died after "falling off a truck," and both of these deaths were "suicides." High-ranking officials' families are now detained in camps until their return when they travel overseas, like to China.

Many of the 11,000 North Koreans who fled to South Korea have testified in recent years about the extensive network of camps. South Korean, Japanese, and Western intelligence have developed a fairly sophisticated understanding of which camps serve which purposes: imprisonment, hard labor, torture, execution, and the like. They do this by comparing their accounts to aerial footage and photographs taken by drones, stealth planes, and satellites. The largest and most well-known camp, Yodok, which is claimed to have been repurposed in 2014 but once housed tens of thousands, if not hundreds of thousands of prisoners, has been likened to the horrors of Auschwitz. Yodok was divided into a "total control zone," a prison camp for persons deemed "enemies of the regime," and a "revolutionary zone," a reeducation camp designed to punish offenders for crimes like criticizing government policy and unlawfully listening to foreign broadcasts. Prisoners who entered the area under strict control never left.

Female North Korean defectors to China are frequently found and brought back to the country while pregnant with a Chinese man's child. The government will often take any action required in these

72

situations to coerce the lady into aborting the fetus. The pregnant lady (or girl, as is frequently the case) will occasionally be injected with a syringe full of an unclean substance, which injures and kills the fetus (and occasionally the mother) as well. In other instances, the pregnant woman is simply kicked till she throws up by jackbooted police or other regime officials, or a wooden board is placed on her abdomen, forcing children to jump on it to crush the unborn. They occasionally place the newborn infant in a box to die if a baby is delivered despite all of this. So is North Korea's "racial purity" preserved.

The North Korean government has long had access to chemical and biological weapons in addition to nuclear ones. Sometimes, people who are considered to be criminals are picked from the general public to take part in "studies" or "experiments" from which they never survive, passing away from toxic gases or contagious diseases that have been weaponized. The Kim dynasty has relied heavily on the supply of scientists, engineers, and other personnel from the Chinese and Russian regimes to keep up these efforts.

North Koreans don't fare much better as citizens even after completing their required military duty. Periodic "collective mobilizations" essentially involve long days of labor, starting with wake-up calls at 5 a.m. and ending with an 8 p.m. return to the home. Back-breaking labor is required, primarily mining in remote coal mines or iron mills. There is no retirement age beyond which one is no longer required to participate, and frequently children as young as ten years old are involved. It is said that "we are all revolutionaries," implying that dying for the regime is a privilege.

I go into great detail about the physical harshness of life in North Korea because that is the only way I can make the point that it is nothing compared to the psychological harm. When I tell people this, they frequently find it difficult to believe me because they question how propaganda on television or agitprop in schools could possibly be worse than genuine incarceration, torture, or execution. Though it is. Every citizen in North Korea is assigned to a small group of other citizens, and every week they all gather to report on and inform each other, confess each other's flaws, accuse each other of wrongdoings, and punish each other through shame and social ridicule. In most places, these sessions are known as "mutual criticism sessions." These gatherings could be severe in rural areas like Kowon, where my mother was born, while they could be intense in towns like Hyesan, my hometown. The residents of this remote, very nationalistic region of the country actually believed they were rebels. There was no resistance, no underground movement, and no freedom warriors. Their dedication to the dictatorship never wavered; they never wavered in their fervor since they had no exposure to the world outside of their country's or even their province's borders.

Every dictatorship has the capacity for abuse and bloodshed. But Kowon's mental servitude continues to represent socialism for me more than torture, incarceration, or corporal punishment.

America's industrial and manufacturing base as well as its supply chains have been eroded by the same American elites who have been selling off their own nation to China for decades. As a result, America is now more vulnerable to external shocks like the pandemic and the conflict in Ukraine. As a result, millions of regular Americans have been thrown into chaos and disaster. Instead of providing assistance to these individuals, elites have stigmatized them as racists, bigots, transphobes, and insurrectionists in order to defend their falling economic standing.

The American people's fundamental goodness, commitment to freedom and liberty, and distrust of authority will probably bring us through. The United States still has some of the strongest constitutional safeguards of any nation in the world. But the conditions have improved enough for a genuine demagogue to take advantage of America's failing institutions, dishonest elites, and growingly despairing lower classes. We have overcome many challenges, including the Great Depression, two major wars, 9/11, the financial crisis of 2008, and the COVID-19 epidemic, but I am concerned about what will transpire the next time a major surprise hits our shores. Will we be able to persevere because of our unity, faith in the rule of law, and assurance in democracy? Or are we going to compromise the Bill of Rights, try to stifle freedom of speech, suppress political opponents, and agree to the government exercising "emergency powers" indefinitely?

Students who buy their way into colleges in North Korea are only taught the correct "political," "socialist" view of medicine, which is why medical care there is so subpar. My right bottom quadrant still bears the scar of socialism from when I was a youngster and was given the incorrect diagnosis of appendicitis when I actually had viral enteritis, which, as I was later informed, would have been simple for any half-trained doctor to identify. Due to years of malnutrition and living on the verge of starvation, I actually carry it all over my body. This scar has affected everything from my capacity to reach a healthy weight to the increased risks of pregnancy and childbirth.

Chapter 12:
Freedom Matters

People frequently question why I didn't take advantage of the chance in America to finally live a private life given the life I had in China and North Korea. Why did I decide to publish books, create videos, and expose myself to the world in such a way that deprives me of any legitimate right to quiet?

The fact is, you never do it with the idea of one day being a well-known person when you first decide to express yourself verbally or in writing to the world. That sort of thing only develops gradually, and it's not until later that the decision's seriousness is apparent. I initially agreed to participate in the South Korean television program Now On My Way to Meet You, but not because I wanted to be a celebrity; rather, I did it because the producers said it was likely my greatest chance in life to get back in touch with my sister.

I didn't really appreciate how little even South Koreans knew about North Korea until I had been on the show for a while. They were really unaware of the extent of the misery occurring beyond their northern border, and when I spoke about it, many people showed sincere compassion and worry. It wasn't that they didn't care or were wilfully ignorant. By the time I received an invitation to the One Young World conference, I had already decided to go. I reasoned that the more people I could inform about North Korea and its people, the higher our chances of bringing about change for the still-victimized population there. I was persuaded to accept the offer of the chance to write a memoir when the video of my speech became widely popular. The same justification served as the inspiration for the YouTube channel. bit by bit, things continued to go on until I eventually found myself being hounded by the Kim dictatorship. My relatives in North Korea were compelled to disparage me on television, and even here in America, I was becoming the target of various forms of harassment, censorship, threats of violence, slander, and con games.

People frequently assume that I must regret making these choices and that I ought to have chosen to live in cozy anonymity here on the vast American continent. There are undoubtedly occasions when it sounds good, but the fact remains that I feel as though my time is running out. I'm 29 years old, but when I look in the mirror and reflect on my life thus far, I feel much older—like I must be close to a thousand. Everything after this point will be viewed as a bonus because the past 29 years have been so full of life and upheaval, love and loss, near misses, and close calls with death. Perhaps there is some melancholy in it, but there is also a sense of liberation. My father passed away without ever experiencing what it was like to be truly free. I was also meant to suffer from that. But I've been bingeing on what he died never having tasted for a while now. I've had enough. I now live solely for my son, for love, and to forward the cause of human rights.

Even years after their escape, the majority of North Korean defectors do not experience feelings like this. My older sister had grown pretty resentful and was still trying to make sense of what had occurred to us up until very recently. She didn't want anyone to know that she was a victim of human trafficking when she was only sixteen, unlike me. She wanted to appear as though she had led a regular life and had no trouble adjusting to a traditional, conservative society like

South Korea's. However, she was straining and irate on the inside. She even changed her name for a while and barred me; for two years, we had no communication. However, I'm happy to report that in the spring of 2022, Eunmi made the decision to start talking about her experiences in China and North Korea, and she is currently learning English so that she may share them more widely. Being her younger sister makes me incredibly proud.

It is impossible, in my opinion, to love America more than I do. However, I would be lying if I didn't admit that it can often be challenging to find that purpose in modern-day America. The emphasis on individuality, "finding your own voice," and "living your own truth" made me a little less naturally compassionate for other people than I had been. I also developed the habit of complaining when things didn't go my way, when people made mistakes, or when circumstances didn't turn out the way I had planned. After only a few years here, I noticed it in my own life.

It's good that so many Americans—including immigrants like myself—have their basic necessities addressed and can thus focus on things like the plushness of hotel beds. However, there is also a risk involved. Few people in America today have ever experienced hunger or have worried about where their next meal will come from. The memory of what it took to create the system of wealth that we take for granted now also fades as the generation that lived through the Great Depression and the two World Wars moves on. America is producing an increasing number of people who want to destroy the system because they don't understand it as it becomes predominantly made up of people who weren't involved in its creation in the first place. They are unaware of how vulnerable their freedom is, how priceless their form of government is, or how uncommon their way of life is. They thus fantasize of demolishing it. These fancies are occasionally coming true.

America is a racist, imperialist, nasty, and greedy nation that bears the greatest share of the blame for world terrorism, war, and other wrongdoings. We won't stop until American capitalism is destroyed, the military and police state are dismantled, and American democracy is revealed for what it really is: a fraudulent facade.

Since it's actually impossible to know, I'm going to venture a guess that you'd place the smallest feasible bet. An ISIS commander or a junior product manager at Twitter may both be the person in question. This has come as quite a shock to someone who has spent equal amounts of time in both worlds—half in the authoritarian government that is hostile to America and half in the United States itself. How did it come to pass that North Korean and American kids were being taught propaganda about the United States that was remarkably similar?

Really, it's no surprise that many Americans who support "social justice" are primarily concerned with the infinite proliferation of incorrect gender pronouns and how much "range" to give chickens before they end up in supermarkets, while millions of people around the world continue to experience murder, starvation, rape, torture, and enslavement. Even though I like to make light of this kind of silly, childish conduct now and again, at the end of the day, it's tragically very serious. A populace becomes vulnerable to exploitation by those in positions of actual power when they lose their connection to history, their grip on reality, and their capacity to comprehend cause and effect.

However, these tiny peripheral notions held by a small number of youngsters and immature adults in isolated enterprises situated in strange regions of the nation can gradually but surely become the prevailing culture of the entire society. Elites in politics, business, and culture will be eager to adopt the new ideology as dogma in all the nation's institutions of power, especially if it benefits them. In some form or another, that process is what took place in North Korea, China, and Russia. In America, a variation of it is currently in progress.

I don't say that to be too dramatic or provocative. Of course, in my opinion, America in 2023 is nothing like North Korea in 1945, China in 1927, or Russia in 1917. I say this solely to emphasize the extremely delicate nature of freedom and civilization, which is the most important lesson I've ever learned in life. Travel the world, and you'll see how indecent most people's lives are in most nations. In many instances, this isn't because a nation has never established a stable social order; rather, it's because any free, tolerant, and reasonably wealthy civilization the nation may have once established was eventually overthrown by an insane individual. Freedom is a precious thing, and its extinction is never more than a generation away, as Ronald Reagan aptly put it. It is not passed down to us by heredity; rather, each generation must continually fight for and maintain it because a nation only receives it once. In addition, people who have had freedom before and lost it have never experienced it again.

When we think of America, we frequently consider July 4, 1776, to be its sole "founding." However, the reality is that America has undergone numerous findings and refoundings over the course of its history. The first founding took place when religious exiles from England founded colonies in the early seventeenth century. These colonists imagined themselves as constructing a New Jerusalem in the New World, practicing self-government under the guidance of God thousands of miles away from the violent and persecuting religious practices of the Old World. The relationship between the colonies and the British Crown, however, deteriorated over the course of more than a century. The British Empire's extended tentacles reached across the Atlantic, depriving the American colonists of their right to self-determination and of equal standing within the British Empire.

The Civil Rights Movement and the New Deal era gave birth to a fourth founding. The bravery of labor organizers battling for the rights of the working class and civil rights activists fighting for equal protection under the law for all races resulted in the nation and society that Americans have since enjoyed. The social contract that this most recent founding kept together, however, has once again begun to fall apart, as it has so frequently in our history. Many American workers no longer have the opportunities they had following the fourth founding due to the shift from an industrial to a digital and services economy, and many capitalist Americans' decisions to export American jobs to China and other countries have left many American workers bitter and dejected. Additionally, racial tensions that dissipated following the successes of the Civil Rights

Movement in the 1960s have returned. And both legal and unauthorized immigration—on a scale not seen since the turn of the 20th century—has poured into the country from Asia and Latin America, adding to the strain on the nation's already troubled social service infrastructure. The comparatively peaceful society of the 1980s and 1990s is now weakened. Americans now distrust one another more than they do their institutions, governmental, and commercial leaders.

It seems obvious that a fifth founding is coming. This situation is serious. The number of wars and civil conflicts since our country's founding has put a strain on our political structure. We frequently only succeeded as a result of the insight, tenacity, and courage of a small number of mighty leaders—a breed of American that is difficult to find in Washington these days. To steer the leaky ship of American self-government over the turbulent waves of the twenty-first century, there is no Washington, no Jefferson, no Lincoln, no Roosevelt, and no King.

For this reason, I think that the restoration of individual accountability and local government will be part of our fifth founding. We have looked to our federal government in Washington, D.C., for far too long to address all of our issues and concerns. However, it is not the president's or the Supreme Court's responsibility to make choices that may affect your family or community. It is our responsibility to engage in daily self-government, not only delegate democratic governance to politicians, as it is yours, mine, and ours.

So attend the city council meetings. Attend the meetings of the local school board. Participate in the homeowners association. Join organizations that bring together people with similar interests. Raise money to attract national artists and performances to your community. Take on a leadership role in your place of worship and assist the less fortunate. Take charge of your kids' sports teams. At the dinner table, discuss America and our shared history with them. At night, read stories to them. Make sure they support their local communities. Don't spend too much time on social media. Limit your consumption of cable news and talk radio. Most of what occurs in Washington should be ignored. Take control of your territory.

The person who first taught me to never, ever give up was my father. He gave me advice to keep moving forward and to find a way to overcome obstacles, even on his deathbed. This man's life had been a nightmare; he had been in and out of jails, frequently starved and tortured, and in his dying days he was suffering from cancer. Because life itself is important, he was the man who advised his young daughter to never give in or submit.

What would my father have thought if he had lived to see America if he had felt that way about the life he led in China and North Korea? He would have undoubtedly considered it to be a miracle. exactly as I do.

Chapter 13:
Warriors of the Light

I started to see a breach in my marriage somewhere in 2019. The ties that had kept us so closely knit when we first got married had started to visibly fray, and by the time we both noticed it, the fraying was irreparably done. We became separated later in 2020, and then we got divorced. Even though I knew it was ultimately for the best, I was nevertheless plagued by the knowledge that I had failed the one thing in life that I had come to care really about—my own family. Was there a problem with me?

Of course, divorce is never easy, and in our case, sharing our wonderful son was a particularly difficult challenge. We made the decision to remain in the same city, to remain equally involved in his life and upbringing, and to do everything in our power to continue instilling the right values in him that my ex-husband and I continued to share as parents to this wonderful child who remained so devoted to him.

I spend a lot of time these days thinking about the values I want to inculcate in my little kid and the types of people I should hold up to him as role models because he is the center of my existence. Compared to other American mothers, I have found this to be harder and less intuitive. I was persuaded that only my own family members were good since I had spent the first half of my life in North Korea and China. Everyone else, I reasoned, was either a liar, a manipulator, or an agent of evil. This is the unavoidable result of learning as a child that there are enemy spies and evil forces everywhere, even among your neighbors and in your own house. I never used to view other people as "role models," as providing a positive example for others, or as reflecting specific beliefs when I was a child. There were only three people: the Dear Leader, who was God, my parents and sister, who were wonderful, and every other person on the planet, who was terrible.

After spending time in South Korea and, in particular, America, I have subsequently been convinced otherwise, but it hasn't been easy for me to approach people with the kind of trust that could come naturally to others. But after meeting some extraordinary people in North America, I've come to see things differently. I now understand that everyone possesses a light and that practically everyone genuinely has the best interests of others in mind; some people simply find it more difficult to do so than others.

Of all the possible paths I may take in life, the one I'm trying to focus on is the defense and advancement of human rights, particularly the right to individual freedom. Because of the hardships I had in my early years, all the pleasures and financial possessions in the world are now meaningless to me unless I can share and enjoy them with individuals who are currently going through the same horrors I did.

Through my life project, I've met people who have similar missions and who broadly agree with how they see their role in the world. These individuals are modern-day freedom fighters who resist the forces of authoritarianism they perceive in their societies and communities and consider it as their duty to serve as positive examples of a free life lived to others. One of my favorite authors, Paulo Coelho, refers to these folks as "warriors of the light." These are typically people who have the intelligence, desire, and ability to live opulent, successful lives in the corporate world, but instead choose to devote their lives to fighting for freedom. I want to thank three people before I end this book since they serve as role models for both my son and me.

My enthusiasm for Dr. Peterson, who has been the woke movement's No. 1 Public Enemy from the start, has grown as the years have passed and I've become the target of more and more attempts at online harassment, "canceling," and the like. He has never let anything stop him from sticking to his guns and being open and honest about his personal beliefs and values. He's become unstoppable and is still more in demand than ever because of his authenticity: You cannot make uninformed listeners, readers, and viewers believe that you hold opinions that you do not. Sincerity is a charming and wonderful trait that elevates you beyond political squabbling and makes the example you set more significant to people than any particular opinion you might have. I think of Dr. Peterson as the embodiment of "realness" everytime I speak in front of a group of people.

When I learned that I had been invited to appear on JRE in Austin, Texas, I was both excited and incredibly anxious. I have previously witnessed interviews where a guest made an effort to display his or her intelligence or accomplishments, and by asking a few simple, sincere questions, Rogan (intentionally or not) exposed their pretension. Friends repeatedly cautioned me not to assume that I didn't need to prepare because Rogan is laid-back, amiable, and fosters a welcoming environment. If you say something that doesn't make sense, sounds incorrect, or that he knows the audience will question, he won't hesitate to bring up the subject, they said.

Sadly, I need not have worried. Before, during, and after the event, Rogan was a model gentleman. I was concerned he would cut it short since I wasn't excellent even though our taped chat ran for more than three hours but seemed to end sooner than I realized. Rogan wasn't interested in "gotchas" or stirring up controversy or making his guest appear foolish or inferior, in contrast to almost every other interviewer I've encountered in popular media. He merely wanted to learn more about the North Korean human rights crisis and China's active role in spreading it because he had heard and read about it but wanted to know more. More than anyone I had ever spoken with, he delved into the intricacies of my escape from North Korea to China and then to South Korea, and I could tell that he was paying close attention and doing so with an open heart as well as an active mind. I recall being particularly struck by the genuineness and casualness with which his questions—which were obviously well-thought-out and prepared—were developed, as if we were just two old friends catching up. Rogan's podcasts may be listened to for three to four hours at a stretch, so it's understandable why those who can only manage brief sound bites from other media outlets enjoy them.

We talked about my time at Columbia, which was my favorite portion of the conversation since Rogan recognized the perils of the woke movement earlier than most people. His key discovery was that because the current generation has never experienced truly difficult circumstances, like all previous generations have, they are able to withstand so little hardship and resort to screaming and wailing so easily. He once said to me, "Hard times create strong men, strong men create good times, good times create weak men, and weak men create hard times" (from G. Michael Hopf's novel Those Who Remain).

Rogan has come under attack from the government and activists because of his propensity to be open and honest, but he has stood his ground, protected his integrity, and remained committed to free speech. I often consider the fundamental decency with which he conducts himself. Being that kind, generous, or sympathetic is difficult. I don't think anyone gets it naturally. To empathize with people as intimately as Rogan does requires effort. It serves as an example that everyone should follow.

Candace Owens was a beautiful person I had the pleasure of meeting as well. After testifying before Congress in 2019 on "confronting white supremacy," Owens emerged as a force of nature. She is an outspoken African-American woman who is not afraid to stick her neck out by refuting critical race theory and extreme antiracism doctrines. Owens uses data to show that very little, if any, of the explanation for crime (even racially motivated crimes) in America is reducible to the "tyranny of the white man." It had a significant impact on my decision to write an account of my own experience. Her memoir, Blackout, is also an emotional narrative of her early upbringing and subsequent political enlightenment. Candace began working at The Daily Wire in 2021, which was co-founded by Ben Shapiro, a conservative commentator and media personality.

Shapiro and I first connected when he featured me on his program near the end of 2020. His stance on a variety of subjects was incredibly interesting to me, notably his now-famous quote, "Facts do not care about your feelings." He also provided insightful commentary on the meritocracy idea and gave listeners counsel that was reminiscent of Jordan Peterson in terms of how to live fulfilled and responsible lives by refusing to place blame for their own predicaments. It goes without saying that I was delighted to receive a request to speak with Candace at The Daily Wire's Nashville headquarters.

I was not let down. The Daily Wire crew was incredibly friendly and courteous. I spent an hour participating in an interview with the social media crew before being directed to another studio where The Candace Owens Show is filmed. Before the segment, I had a brief encounter with her and as a thank-you, I gave her a signed copy of In Order to Live.

She was a very skilled interviewer who probed deeply about my time in North Korea, the circumstances of my escape, and the challenges I faced in China. We also discussed several similarities that we both agreed exist in modern American society. Owens was taken aback when her audience stood up to applaud the two of us at the conclusion of the interview. Evidently, such had never occurred before in the history of the program.

I can still picture myself sitting there next to Candace Owens, a young Black woman, with a thick North Korean accent, taking in the mixed audience's cheers and smiles. This is America, I told myself.

Printed in Great Britain
by Amazon

27914149R00048